babies *from the* heart

a complete guide to adoption

babies *from the* heart

a complete guide to adoption

Nandini Sengupta

EBURY PRESS

An imprint of Penguin Random House

EBURY PRESS

USA | Canada | UK | Ireland | Australia
New Zealand | India | South Africa | China | Singapore

Ebury Press is part of the Penguin Random House group of companies whose addresses can be found at global.penguinrandomhouse.com

Published by Penguin Random House India Pvt. Ltd
4th Floor, Capital Tower 1, MG Road,
Gurugram 122 002, Haryana, India

Penguin Random House India

First published by Random House India 2011

10 9 8 7 6 5 4 3 2

ISBN 9788184001907

Typeset in Berling by Pen2print Media Solution, Okhla

Printed at Manipal Technologies Limited, India

www.penguin.co.in

FSC www.fsc.org MIX Paper | Supporting responsible forestry FSC® C043100

This is a legitimate digitally printed version of the book and therefore might not have certain extra finishing on the cover.

To my darling, Kiki
Thank you for choosing me to be your Mamma

Contents

Foreword

Oprah Winfrey once said, 'Biology is the least of what makes someone a mother.' Anyone can give birth. That's biology. But it takes a lot of blood, sweat, tears, and smiles to be a Mum.

Anyone who has experienced it knows that being a mum is no piece of cake. It's messy, tiresome, and exhausting. But it's also uplifting, exhilarating, and life-affirming. It makes us complete. It makes us want to be a better human being.

I have always wanted to be a mother. After I won the Miss Universe crown, my humanitarian duties included projects for children. It isn't surprising that my winning answer—'The origin of a child is a mother, a woman; woman is sharing, she shows a man what sharing, caring, and loving is all about'—was on the essence of a woman. To me, my role as a mother to my two beautiful girls, Renee and Alisah, is the one that I cherish the most.

Don't get me wrong, I love my job. But beyond the rough and tumble of a life under the arc lights lies the joy of coming home to my babies. Of sharing chocolates and confidences. Of good night tales and naughty corners. Of school work and home play. The little nameless unremembered acts that make me who I am. It's my ultimate elixir.

That's probably why I chose to became a mother so early. I am a successful actress but I didn't want my career or the search for a partner to come in the way of my desire to be a mother. I wanted to experience the highs and lows, I wanted to hold my baby in my arms and watch her fall asleep listening to the rhythm of my heartbeat. I knew life would find me my ideal partner when the time is right. But I didn't want to wait for the ideal moment to be a mother. For me, the right time was now. That's why I chose to be a mother from the heart. I chose adoption.

My decision to adopt was in many ways a huge learning experience. Parenting is never easy. And adoptive parenting much less so. Having gone through the process of adopting two little girls, I now know what scores of parents, particularly single mums like me, go through when they sign up for adoption. There's plenty of paperwork that needs to be taken care of, the legal process is also a bit lengthy, there are huge amounts of rules and regulations that you need to abide by and of course, when it's time for disclosure, you need to answer your child with honesty and love. Nothing else will do.

That's why I am happy that a book like *Babies from the Heart* will now be available to all those adoptive parents who don't know where to start their search for parenthood. A handy guide about the legal, procedural, emotional, medical, and other aspects of adoptive parenting is both timely and absolutely necessary. It's also touching that the book takes its title from something I told my daughter Renee many years ago. When she asked me if she was born from my tummy, I told her, 'You were born from my heart.'

Adoptive parenting is all about that special bond. It's a bond born from the heart, and *Babies from the Heart* celebrates that bond, gently handholding first-time parents through the process. An adoptive parent herself, the author handles the subject with personal warmth. I wish I had something like this to turn to when I first became a proud adoptive mother. Ask any mum, adoptive or biological, and she'll tell you motherhood has little to do with genes. It's about love—heartfelt, true, and tender. It's about putting your child first, always. It's about thinking outside of yourself. It's about holding on. It's about letting go. That's the essence of being a mother. That's also the essence of being a woman.

I should know. I am both.

Sushmita Sen
August, 2011
Mumbai

Preface

When Kiki, our beautiful adopted baby girl, our bundle of joy and the love of my life, first came home more than three years ago, she turned our lives upside down and inside out. Back then, we found ourselves turning increasingly to fellow adoptive parents in our wider circle of friends and acquaintances—people who could give us valuable tips on what to do and how to do it, and how to make sense of the jumble of emotions we were going through. A number of friends offered help with the choice of the agency; others gave tips on how to handle the tricky issue of biologic versus adoptive parents; and still others offered help and information on the legal process of becoming adoptive parents.

That handholding was invaluable for us because it prepared us for the most important and challenging role of our lives and gave us some parameters to measure everything by. It's a little bit like asking your mum, aunt, and other members of the family about what to expect when you're expecting and how best to enjoy your baby once she's born. In the case of adoptive parents, there are aspects to parenting which only other adoptive parents can help out with and that's how the idea of this book was born.

I have been researching for this book for nearly two years, talking to adoptive parents, prospective adoptive parents, and even couples who, for reasons of their own, decided not to go in for adoption. As more and more couples, both double-income-no-kids variety like us as well as those who already have biological children, opt for adoption, a handy guide to adoptive parenting looked like a very good idea. All the answers to the issues raised in this book have been culled either from our own experience as parents or from the experiences of one or more of the couples I spoke to while researching this book. I have, for the sake of the privacy of some of the couples interviewed for this book, changed the names of both the parents as well as the child. These names have been marked with an asterisk. However, I have left the names unchanged in those cases where the couples were okay with being quoted.

I have also consulted experts Professor Daniel Close, University of Oregon; Vinita Bhargava, author of *Adoption in India: Policies and Experiences*; Deborah D. Gray, author of *Attaching in Adoption*; and Lois Ruksai Melina, author of *Raising Adopted Children*. I am deeply indebted to them.

I would like to thank every single adoptive parent I have spoken to while researching for this book. Interacting with so many wonderful parents, hearing your stories, sharing your lives as it were, has been an incredible experience. I truly believe these interactions have helped me become a better, more understanding, less confused parent, as indeed I hope they will help the readers of this book.

I would also like to thank the Random House team for their help, constant handholding, and clarity of vision on how they wanted this book to shape up. I am immensely grateful to my husband who has been patiently pestering me for years to 'get on with the book' and my mother from whom I liberally borrow ideas on parenting. And last but not the least, I would like to thank my dear friend Reshmi Dasgupta for her unstinted help in getting me a wider circle of couples to talk to, and simply doing everything she could to make this book become more than just an idea in my head.

Babies from the Heart is not an empirical exercise. It is a heartfelt effort at trying to make sense of what's certainly the most wonderful experience of our lives. If it helps even a single parent, answers a single query, or allays a single doubt, I will consider my job well done.

Happy parenting!

1

The Decision

WHEN MY HUSBAND and I first decided to adopt a baby girl, we felt it was an intensely personal decision and needed to stay that way. So for a while, no one but our immediate family and a couple of close friends knew that we had taken 'the decision'.

Big mistake. Why? Let me explain. Our first step was to Google the names of adoption agencies in our city (we were living in Delhi at that time) and make a list of numbers to call. But we quickly found out, to our exasperation, that many of those numbers simply did not exist or were obviously wrongly listed. (Things are easier now with the Central Adoption Resource Authority or CARA as it is more popularly known. CARA lists the phone numbers of relevant agencies city-wise and offers the option of online registration). Meanwhile acquaintances gave wrong or misleading information confusing us even more. My gym friend said, 'Get in touch with a nursing home and you'll get your baby. . .all you need to do is pay Rs 100,000 if you want a girl and Rs 200,000 if you want a boy.' What I didn't know is that this route is risky and illegal. My gym friend is not an adoptive parent herself and so was passing on hearsay as information.

In the meantime after several tries, we got through to the Civil Lines number of Missionaries of Charity and that's where we took an appointment and signed up. Six months later, we were still waiting for a call. We met the good sisters at Missionaries and they said there was a long queue and we may have to wait a while longer. That's when we did what we should have done much earlier—calling fellow adoptive parents and asking them for advice. Within a week, we got some good options—check with agencies in other cities particularly in smaller towns, check with other reputed agencies in Delhi like Palna, work out a timeline for yourselves, get a fix on how long you're prepared to wait for the baby, and then take a call. Fortunately for us, we didn't need to exercise Plans B, C, or D—we got a call from our agency mid-February and took our baby home a week later. But right from then on, we realized that four heads—or more—are better than two when it comes to parenting.

The choice of agency is only one aspect on which we sought advice but there are several other questions that would-be adoptive parents came up with during the course of researching this book. Most couples nurture an ideal in their head about their parenting experiences and reconciling that ideal with reality is one of the biggest tasks for first-time parents. In the case of adoptive parenting that task starts with dealing with the issue of infertility or sorting out the reason why you want to adopt in the first place.

When to Consider Adoption

One of the questions that kept popping up as I interviewed prospective adoptive parents for this book was if it is okay to go for adoption even if we're not 100 percent sure we can't have biological kids. Rana* and Romona* tried for years to have a baby and finally decided to adopt a little girl. However, just days after the baby came home, Romona discovered she was pregnant. With Pronnoy* and Jayanti*, their biological son was born three years after their adopted daughter came home. Although there's no scientific evidence to support this, adoptive parents are often blessed with a biological child as well and fertility experts say the reason is because once parents, couples are less pressured about having a baby. Even popular culture mirrors this—Sex and the City's

Charlotte and her husband Harry adopted their little girl Lily from China and soon afterwards had a biological daughter Rose.

Yet in six out of ten couples considering adoption that I spoke to, the prospect of having a biological child was the biggest reason for their indecision. In other words, they wanted to be sure they couldn't have biological children before they made up their mind about adoption. Or were confused about whether it was okay to sign up for adoption even if they weren't sure about not being able to have biological children in future. The truth is that couples who have both adopted and biological kids say that's the best mix possible. (This subject is discussed in greater detail in Chapter 11: Biological and Adoptive Mixed Households). The siblings look out for each other with the biological child trying to protect his adopted sibling from insensitive remarks in school or in the play group. Also, explaining the difference between being adopted and biological or even breaking the news that she's adopted to the child becomes easier when there's a sibling to share the emotional tumult.

Increasingly, there are parents with one or more biological children who are still looking to adopt a baby. Although the law does not discriminate against couples with children, some agencies actively prefer childless couples. Given the grave mismatch between the number of children legally available for adoption and the huge queue of parents who sign up for a baby, some agencies feel a childless couple should get first preference, followed by couples with children and finally single parents. So in case you already have biological children and are looking to adopt, check their preferences with the agency of your choice.

Either way the decision to adopt is perhaps the most important and life-changing decision that a couple can take. So if there's any doubt, it's best to wait some more. Even if the couple is convinced but the immediate family would still prefer a biological child, it may be best to wait a bit longer and bring them around. After all, these will be lifelong relationships for the child and any doubt can have a seriously crippling effect. It can even lead to teenage delinquency and other behavioural issues in the future.

In our case, though childless, we were not really concerned about the biological clock. We wanted to adopt our baby and did. Others like Probir* and Madhumita* took a cue from her sister who already had an adopted baby. They signed up for a child within a couple of years of getting married.

Couples who conceive after adopting a child, though, should be ready for unintentionally insensitive remarks from friends and family. Rana and Romona, for example, had elderly aunts clucking in dismay saying, 'If only you had waited a little while longer before adopting... now you have your own baby...' The best way to fob off such gratuitous remarks is to say, 'Sure, now we will have two children of our own...someone up there must have decided we're good parent material.'

In her seminal book *Raising Adopted Children: A Manual for Adoptive Parents*, Lois Ruskai Melina talks about likely 'disharmony' as the extended family adjusts to the adopted child. 'Extended family members have to welcome the new family member, too often without adequate preparation or a thorough understanding of adoptive relationships. There is likely to be some disharmony as family members learn how the addition of the new child affects them,' she writes.

Often the remarks are not meant to be deliberately hurtful and are actually intended as a compliment. My husband and I routinely face effusive reactions like, 'It's so noble of you to do this' or 'if every couple in this country did what you have done, we would not need orphanages'. The problem with statements like these is that they can be incredibly offensive to the adopted child. So if the off-the-cuff hurtful remarks are made in the presence of the adopted child who is old enough to understand them, you'll need to cut short the remark AND explain the biological/adopted issue to the child in a manner that justifies the reason why you adopted. You'll need to be careful while doing this because parents can go overboard while explaining this tricky issue and end up window dressing it too much. The idea is to give the facts, not in a negative manner but in simple terms. (This issue is discussed in greater detail in Chapter 4: When to Talk Adoption). For instance, instead of saying, 'We wanted a precious angel and we chose you' or 'Daddy and Mummy were sad because we couldn't be parents so we went to the agency to have you', you could say, 'Daddy and Mummy really wanted to be parents and the sisters/agency helped us to find you.' That way you don't tell the child that she was chosen because her parents were NOT able to have a biological child. Nor does she think she's in any way special or different because she's adopted.

The Trigger: What Makes Us Adopt

For many childless couples not interested in going for infertility treatments, adoption is not the best but the only option to become parents. Yet adoptive parents are not always the desperate couples of popular imagination.

Monica and Chandler's shenanigans (from the popular sitcom, FRIENDS) may be good TV but it is hardly real. In our case, my husband and I were childless for about 14 years before we decided to adopt. Many fellow adoptive parents often ask us, 'What took you so long?' The truth is we did want a baby in our lives but all through our 20s and early 30s we were perfectly content with our social and professional lives and simply did not have time or mind space to think about a child. By the time we started thinking, we were already in our 30s and it took us another couple of years to get used to the idea of becoming parents. In a sense we took time to get used to the idea of a baby—biological or adopted. And after a couple of years we felt adopting a child was much better than going through costly and difficult infertility treatments.

There are many DINK couples who, like us, take time to adopt. But there are just as many couples who decide on adoption within a couple of years of getting married and sometimes after having biological children. The trigger can be wanting to have a girl child, wanting to have a child very late (like the Cutinhas) or wanting to get around a medical/genetic problem that cannot be solved even by infertility treatments (Arun* and Shonali*).

Most adoptive parents admit that the real trigger behind their decision is often a beautiful adopted baby in their immediate circle. After Lancelot and Sheela Cutinha adopted baby Brigitte, it prompted six of their friends to follow suit, not all of them childless. In fact, many parents I spoke to admitted that their decision to adopt was jump-started by their friend/colleague/neighbour's beautiful adopted baby but were worried that they were being facile about such a crucial decision. Are parents overreacting or is it wrong to base such a profound decision as parenting on superficial triggers like these?

It took Arun and Shonali more than six years to come around to the idea of adoption. Shonali's fragile health and several miscarriages finally convinced them that they wanted a baby from the heart. Being close friends and neighbours, they also came home often and were charmed by our little girl. Shonali would often say, 'I'd like my baby girl to have Kiki's big smile.' They signed up for adoption two years ago but remained childless till they finally decided to change their agency. Earlier this year, they finally became parents of Baby Aleya*. So what happened?

Arun and Shonali went by word of mouth advice and signed up with a well-known Delhi-based agency. Nearly everyone they talked to told them it was perhaps the best in the region; yet their experience turned out to be far from pleasant. An extremely good looking couple, they wanted a baby that fitted their racial profile. So they turned down the first child offered to them. The second one seemed perfect. The couple were over the moon except when they took her for a medical examination, the paediatrician recommended a torch test. The results showed that she had congenital cytomegalovirus (CMV) infection which if symptomatic could cause all kinds of abnormalities either now or in future including hearing deficiency which she was already showing signs of. CMV infections in newborn babies are rare—only 1–2 percent get it and only around 10 percent of these infections show up symptoms, says the *Indian Journal for the Practising Doctor*. But those who do, have a 20–30 percent mortality rate. Apart from a relatively high mortality rate, it can cause hearing problems, mental retardation, and potentially fatal neonatal illnesses like pneumonia and hepatitis.

Meanwhile the couple complained that the agency was getting stroppy and that it was all becoming a bit unpleasant. I told them what I would tell any prospective adoptive parent—most agencies take a very dim view of what they call 'baby shopping'. The ever-smiling Sister Anthea, in charge of Missionaries of Charity's Delhi chapter, puts it beautifully. 'When you have a biological child, do you love her any less because she doesn't look the way you imagined she would? You don't love her any less because she's fat or thin, short or tall, dark or fair. The adopted child is as much a gift from above as a biological one. So why should you nitpick about one and not the other?'

Legally, the agency is supposed to make 'best efforts to assign a child as per required description' given by the parents, according to the government's new guidelines for in-country adoption. But most experts on adoption and adoptive parents agree that opting for adoption because you want the perfect baby is a really bad idea. No baby is perfect—either biological or adopted. Interestingly most adopted babies, after a while, tend to look like their parents. My daughter, for instance, is the spitting image of my mother and Arun and Shonali's just-adopted baby girl resembles her maternal grandfather. Agencies try their best to match the baby with the racial profile of its prospective parents. For instance, Eron* and Pritha Vaughn*, a mixed race couple, have been blessed with their beautiful baby Lily* who is also of obviously mixed parentage. But the match is also subject to availability and couples looking to adopt should respect and appreciate this.

Asking for a Profile Match

Many prospective adoptive parents feel anxious that the baby given to them will not match their racial profile.

The law says that the agency will try to match a child with the 'required description' desired by the parents. And to the extent possible, agencies try to do just that, looking for north Indian babies for north Indian parents and if possible mixed race babies for mixed race parents. That's part of the reason why very often adopted kids bear a striking resemblance to their parents or grandparents. The other reason has to do with cultural conditioning. The presentability factor depends as much on grooming and cultural upbringing as on basic physical traits. That's probably the reason why adopted children look like their parents or extended family. As they grow up and share their family values, it not only builds their habits and character but also determines the way they look. And this starts a lot earlier than teens by when the child has a more significant contribution to her look and her choice of wardrobe.

Sometimes though, it is not possible to get a perfect match. In such cases there may be some mismatch between what the parents expected and what the agency could offer. Parents themselves may have some very practical reasons for being choosy. In the case of Arun and Shonali, for instance, they felt a profile match would give the child a better footing with the extended family. 'If the extended family did not accept the child, it would be a big problem in future so we wanted as close a profile match as possible,' said Shonali. That's what prompted the pair to say no to the first baby offered to them. The second time round, the baby had serious medical problems so the agency took her back. Most agencies make it very clear to the prospective parents that they would be perfectly willing to take the baby back if the child does not meet the parents' expectations. However, that basically refers to medical problems—indeed when Probir and Madhumita took their adopted baby Preeti to the paediatrician, the initial tests indicated some hearing deficiency. Later, more tests cleared the doubt and it turned out to be nothing more serious than ear wax. However, adopted babies can and often do have serious congenital problems apart from malnutrition and other health issues and prospective parents should be prepared for all manner of medical surprises. Most adoptive parents I spoke to, though, felt even medical complications were no reason to give up the child. A detailed report from the paedetrician simply helps the new parents be better prepared for any medical eventuality.

Choosing the Baby

That said, to-be parents often want to know if they will be allowed to 'choose' a baby. Technically, prospective parents have the right to take a look at the nursery and indicate their preference and many agencies allow you to do so. Parents also have the right to say no to a baby if they are not happy with the child's medical condition or profile match. According to Dr Jagannath Pati, deputy director and public information officer, CARA, an agency is supposed to show prospective parents up to three babies as options. The new guidelines say if the parents reject these three options, they will then need to wait for three months before they are eligible once again.

All agencies offer parents the option of returning the baby in case the medical examination throws up some unexpected complications as in the case of Arun and Shonali's baby. So the parents do have a choice but the choice has to be exercised judiciously.

In nine out of ten parents I spoke to, though, the first child shown to them was the one they took home. In most cases the first glimpse of the child is an extremely emotional moment for the parents. Most parents don't even offer a checklist though they are asked about the gender and age at the time of registering for adoption. As Madhumita puts it so beautifully, 'We offered no checklist because we wanted to take the child destined for us. So we left it to the sisters at Missionaries.' If you want, you will be allowed to take a look at the children in the nursery but many parents choose not to.

Either way, the first day, first look is a moment no parent ever forgets. Probir and Madhumita, for instance, fell in love with baby Preeti the moment they first saw her. As the baby gurgled in her father's arms, her parents had a moment of epiphany. 'It was a barrage of emotions and we knew life would never be the same again... it was life summarized in a minute,' says Madhumita. I remember going through the same tumultuous emotions when we first saw Kiki and she instinctively grabbed my husband's little finger. Later when we carried her to the chapel for a simple prayer beautifully conducted by the sisters, both of us had tears in our eyes. Having a baby is a life-in-a-minute moment for all parents, adoptive or biological.

Specifying the Gender and Age of the Baby

The law allows prospective parents to specify their preferences to the agency of their choice. In our case, for instance, we specified that we wanted a baby girl and that we wanted the child to be as young as possible. As a result, Kiki came home at two months and ten days. In the case of Sudha* and Purab*, they wanted an older child and got a six-month-old baby. There are pros and cons to adopting both very small infants or a slightly older child. (This subject is discussed in greater detail in Chapter 9: Adopting an Older Child). One common problem that parents face when taking home an older infant is that the baby takes longer to adapt to the new environment and often takes at least a year to shake off its neonatal under-nutrition. Indeed parents sometimes have to wait for a year or more before the baby gains weight enough to get past the underweight or borderline underweight mark. In the case of very small infants, too, there are problems like we discovered. Often infections don't show up so early but parents may face a full-blown medical emergency within weeks of the baby coming home. In our case, Kiki went from being a healthy baby to one with galloping pneumonia within 48 hours and had to be hospitalized. She was in neonatal intensive care for a fortnight before recovering fully and coming home to us. It was a traumatic time both for her as well as for us, a baptism by fire of sorts. So if you're taking home a very small baby, you can expect nasty surprises like these as well. Legally though you can adopt a baby as small as two months old and as old as five or six years old. Most agencies say adoption of children older than five or six years is not encouraged in India because the child then finds it very difficult to fit into his new environment. The new guidelines just released by CARA specify that no child who is seven years old or more, 'who can understand and express his or her opinion, shall be declared legally free for adoption without his or her consent'. The government guidelines say older children should give either a written consent or a verbal one or offer a thumb impression to show they understand they're being given in for adoption and are okay with it.

How to Choose the Agency

CARA lists the approved agencies city-wise complete with phone numbers so that's a good place to start. When Eron and Pritha Vaughn decided to adopt, they checked out the numbers listed under CARA's Delhi list where they were posted at that time. They registered with four agencies, all of which said it would take at least a year for them to get their baby. Eventually, it took a lot less time though the procedure was complicated since Eron, a foreign national, had by then been posted overseas (This subject is discussed in greater detail in Chapter 8: The Legal Angle). However, the couple was happy enough with their choice of agency to now consider returning to them for their second adopted baby.

Although CARA's new, improved website is a good place to start, our personal experience and that of all the parents I spoke to for this book convinced me that word of mouth is the best way to choose an agency. As many as three sets of adoptive parents in our wider circle of friends rooted for Missionaries of Charity so that's where we signed up. Others like Arun and Shonali took the cue from adoptive parents in their circle of friends before signing up and getting their baby from Children of the World in Delhi. Still others like Rupali Mitra* rooted for Shreevatsa, the adoption arm of Society of Friends of Sassoon Hospital (SOFOSH) in Pune while Jayanti and Pronnoy Gupta have turned the Delhi-based Palna into a generic for adopted babies while explaining the process to their daughter.

During the course of my interviews for this book, I came across parents often stumbling across their ideal agency. Take Lancelot Cutinha and his wife Sheela. Already blessed with two beautiful biological girls, the couple adopted their youngest daughter Brigitte from the Holy Cross Home for Babies, Amravati. Reason: they 'realized that in small towns, adoption happens on fast track'. The couple got their baby in three months flat although the legal proceedings took a little while longer. Ditto with Sumit* and Radhika Bawa* who decided to adopt their baby girl from Kolkata because back then (more than fifteen years ago) the procedures were simpler in that part of the country.

CARA's new guidelines say parents should register with one recognized adoption agency close to where they live. They can register online at www.adoptionindia.nic.in. In case the parents want to adopt from an agency other than the one that they have registered with, they will need to approach the Adoption Coordinating Agency (ACA) or State Adoption Resource Agency (SARA) with their registration slip. The ACA or SARA will then contact the agency that the parents wish to adopt from so that they are immediately included in the waiting list. Similarly, if you wish to adopt from an agency in another state, you'll need to approach the ACA or SARA of that state with your registration slip for a similar process.

One word of advice though—before signing up, make sure you talk to as many adoptive parents as possible. It's entirely possible that two sets of people may give completely contradictory pictures of the same agency depending on their personal experience. So contact the adoptive parents in your wider circle of friends and acquaintances, ask them about their experiences; talk about what the social worker will ask in the home study report and how best to field her questions; ask them what the legal procedure is and what kind of preparation you need to make before the baby comes home. Unlike biological parents, adoptive parents don't get nine months to prepare themselves and the family for the arrival of their child. These interactions are therefore crucial for the parents. Typically, many agencies actually ask prospective parents if they know of other adoptive parents. Having an adopted child in the immediate family is considered a plus point—it's a sign that the extended family is comfortable with the idea of adoption. Those who don't have any adopted nephews or nieces—like us—can talk about friends who have adopted and quote their experience in the home study. Of course, as parents you are perfectly within your rights to change your agency if you are unhappy with the services offered. You should also check your rights and responsibilities with the CARA centre to prevent any arm-twisting by the agency. In the case of Shivi and Mannat*, their relationship with the agency hit such a low that they were threatened with blacklisting. However, CARA's public information officer Dr Jagannath Pati clarifies that there is no such centralised list of prospective parents and agencies cannot summarily blacklist a couple on their own. CARA will need to know the details of the case before they are allowed to take any such action.

Adoption Criteria: Age, Financial Eligibility, Marital Status

There is an age limit for couples looking to adopt. According to CARA, which comes under the Union Ministry of Women and Child Development, Government of India, the sum total of the couple's age should not exceed 90 years if the parents are looking to adopt an infant in the 0–3 years age group with neither parent being more than 50 or less than 25 years old. For older children (above 3 years of age), the age limit for parents is relaxed a wee bit—the couple's age in that case goes up to 105 years with neither partner being less than 25 or more than 55 years old. For single parents, CARA specifies a 30–50 year age bracket. Of course, the age factor can and often is relaxed depending on how strong your case is.

The age limit, for instance, may be relaxed in the case of special needs children or single parents who otherwise fulfil all other criteria. In the case of special needs children (which include older children as well as siblings), CARA's new guidelines say that 'older and experienced parents tend to be more committed to parent a child with special needs and thus are more likely to have the skills, patience, financial means, and parenting experience...' The guidelines also add that parents who through their field of work or exposure to the specific medical condition of the child may also be better equipped to handle a special needs child. All of these will be considered during the home study report.

According to CARA guidelines, the eligibility criteria are uniform no matter which state the agency is in. Prospective parents should not be more than 50 years old, couples should have been married for at least two years and they should be in excellent physical and mental health. CARA specifies that prospective parents should not be suffering from 'any contagious or terminal disease or any such mental or physical condition which may prevent them from taking care of the child'. The agency will require a medical certificate as an assurance of health and there have been instances of couples being denied a child on health grounds, particularly that of the mother.

Some agencies, though, have their own additional rules. For instance, some will insist on a certificate from the gynaecologist/family physician saying that the couple could not have a biological child due to a particular medical condition. (CARA, however, clearly states that an infertility statement is *not* required for adoption). Others ask for a no objection certificate from the grandparents. (This too is *not* required). Prospective parents often find these additional criteria objectionable and since they are not part of the law of the land, can justifiably put their foot down if they feel strongly about it.

The other critical criterion is financial eligibility. According to CARA, the parent 'should have adequate financial resources to provide a good upbringing to the child'. The new guidelines also instruct the social workers conducting the home study report to check out the standard of living and the amenities in the couple's home. Besides, prospective parents now need to cough up considerably more than before if they want to adopt. For instance, they need to pay Rs 1000 to register with an agency and another Rs 5000 as home study report and follow-up service fees. Once the adoption is through, parents will need to pay the agency Rs 40,000 towards the child care corpus. The nearly Rs 50,000 bill means that the parents need to be financially stable enough to afford a baby. Earlier though, most agencies depended on donations from happy parents rather than a structured fee. I still remember we paid nothing more than a small sum towards legal expenses. By making the contributions more structured, though, the guidelines will give agencies more elbow room and enough resources for facilities.

The agencies themselves have their own parameters to measure financial stability of prospective parents. According to Sister Anthea of Missionaries of Charity, most agencies have their own financial criteria—a monthly income of around Rs 15,000–20,000 along with a self-owned house is considered adequate—and sometimes the judge may also have her own set of rules to measure prospective parents by. In many cases, the judge is known to have taken a monthly income of Rs 25,000 per month as the minimum cut-off for eligibility. Either way, agencies say they accept 'comfortable living conditions' as a base while determining eligibility criteria. In Missionaries, for instance, education levels of the parents are equally if not more important than just financial eligibility. The home study report in fact includes details of educational qualifications.

As for marital status, most agencies demand that couples produce a marriage certificate (which puts live-in partners firmly out of the race). CARA's new guidelines clearly say live-in couples cannot adopt. Indeed, agencies often also question couples on the status of their relationship—you can expect questions on this issue during the home study visit by the social worker—and expect parents to keep them in the loop if there's any marital discord simmering in the background. The idea is that the child should go to a happy, healthy, normal environment, not a home fraught with tension between the parents.

Along with medical certificates—from a family doctor vouchsafing that the parents are physically and mentally fit to rear a child—and your marriage documents, you will also need letters of reference from friends and family as part of the adoption procedure.

CARA lists the following documents that parents must arm themselves with before taking their baby home in foster care:

- Proof of identity (voter card, PAN card, driver's licence);
- Proof of address which clearly shows residence in India for more than a year;
- Marriage certificate;
- Family photograph;
- A health certificate to guarantee that the parents are not suffering from any terminal or contagious disease and are in good shape mentally and physically to be able to take care of the child;
- Two letters of recommendation from people who know the couple well but are not from among immediate members of the extended family;
- If self-employed, IT statements for three years or an income certificate from the employer indicating the date of retirement;

- Bank statements for the last six months, details of movable or immovable property and loans which the couple may have taken;
- The adoption decree if the couple have adopted before along with written consent of the adopted or biological children if they are older than seven years;
- Divorce or legal separation decree for single parents if applicable;
- A letter from a close relative of the adoptive parents stating that in case of 'any unforeseen circumstances' the relative would take care of the child;
- Passport copy.

Eligibility of Single Parents

Under the law, single parents in the 30–50-year age bracket are eligible for adoption. If the parent wants to adopt an infant in the 0–3 age group, she cannot be more than 45 or less than 30 years old. In the case of older children, that norm is relaxed but the parent still has to be between 30 and 50 years of age. Like couple adoptees, single parents should also have financial stability and additional family support system to help bring up the child.

Although the law does not discriminate, many agencies prefer couples to single parents simply because they believe a couple household offers a more traditional and complete home environment for the child. In the case of couples undergoing separation or divorce, the marital status needs to be clearly mentioned while applying for adoption. Celebrity single parent adoptees like Sushmita Sen or Sandeep Soparkar have an easier time because of the attendant media attention on their decision to adopt. Non-celeb single parents may need to agency hop or wait a little longer to get their child. Also, the law says that single adoptive fathers don't get a baby girl. Placing a child with same sex couples is also not allowed by law. There's no such rule for single mothers. Single parents may stand a better chance of getting a baby if they opt for an older child or a special needs child.

Most agencies, though, lay special emphasis on the home infrastructure in the case of single parents. The home study for instance could include questions on caregivers if the single parent is also a working one. So if you are a prospective single adoptive parent, you should have the entire caregiver infrastructure—grandparents, aunts, cousins as well as domestic help—down pat to be able to convince the social worker that the child's upbringing will not be affected by the lack of one parent.

Getting the Spouse on Board

Niyati and Kartik* have been married for ten years. They have long been trying to have a baby and Niyati has been going through fertility treatments for the past two years. She's had several miscarriages, the last being as recent as the summer of 2010. Tired of the treatment, the multiple miscarriages, and the whole process of waiting to become a mother, Niyati is really keen on adopting a baby. But Kartik is unconvinced.

Getting your partner on board is the first and most significant step in the road to becoming adoptive parents. A reluctant or disinterested partner can skew your chances of getting the baby—social workers typically insist on speaking to the couple to check if both are equally eager and that's one of the crucial aspects of the home study. And if by some chance you do manage to get through the home study, a disinterested/reluctant parent can play havoc on the child's psyche. Take the case of Anondo* and Mala*. A divorcee with a bad marriage behind him, Anondo really wanted to start a family quickly. Already in his mid-40s, he desperately wanted to adopt. Having an adorable adopted niece only convinced him more. But his wife, who's from a different cultural milieu, was not convinced. Anondo took her to visit all the reputed adoption centres in his city (Kolkata) but Mala still wanted a biological child. Result: three years on, the couple are still childless. The adoption issue put such a strain on the relationship that Anondo and Mala are currently separated.

Getting your partner to simply 'agree' to the idea of adoption isn't enough. The couple should be on the same wavelength to make the whole experience of parenting beautiful and conducive to the child's development. In most cases where an indifferent or even reluctant partner came around, the change of mind was triggered by close proximity to an adopted child in the family or immediate friends' circle. Take Probir and Madhumita. Probir loves cats, is devoted to his family, and is a generally amiable character. But he's never been overly fond of very small kids. An intellectual, he likes them when they are able to respond and interact with him. But after his marriage to Madhumita, Probir became very close to his niece, Pompey*. Daughter of Madhumita's sister, the chirpy and playful Pompey helped Probir get 'a hang of babies' and when the couple got their own adopted baby sometime later, Probir became an enthusiastic and hands-on dad, wanting to share the whole experience of parenting with his wife from feeds to toilet training to playtime with their baby.

To be perfectly honest I can completely understand Probir's transformation because I am a living example of how quickly a baby can change a person. I have never been a baby person, never felt like instinctively coochie-cooing to every baby in my vicinity, have always preferred slightly older children with whom I could have a conversation. Newborn babes, to me, were kinda subhuman...although cute, all they did was eat, sleep, and pee, none of which excited me very much. Even when our baby first came home, I would be wracked by guilt wondering if I'll ever be able to 'take to' her. But I did and she took to me too. It's just a question of building a bond and it takes time. Access to an adopted child makes that whole process easier and quicker.

Having said that, it's best to wait till your spouse comes around rather than force the idea of a child on him. It's not good for the marriage and it can be very bad for the child. In the case of Pompey, for instance, her parents separated soon after her adoption and the child has grown up in a single-parent household. Having an uncle, aunt, and an extended family almost next door helped her get over the feeling of being a single-parent child. Without that support structure, Pompey would not have turned out as confident as she is.

Waiting for the Baby

Because of the long queue of prospective adoptive parents, the wait is often longer than you would prefer. In our case, we signed up in August and got our child in February. In the case of Probir and Madhumita, for instance, the wait was much shorter and little Preeti came home within a couple of months of her parents signing up. However, CARA guidelines clearly say that parents have the right to know the reason for delay if there is no response from the agency within two or three months of signing up. The new guidelines clearly say that the agency will need to prepare a home study report within two months of registration for within the country adoptions. At any rate, the would-be parents will go through the home study report within a maximum of four months of registration. The agency will also continuously update parents on the status of their application. Even without the guidelines, agencies, typically, warn parents upfront about the wait. In our case, we were told that we may have to wait as long as six–eight months but our baby came home before that. It's a good idea for parents to be pro-active and stay in touch with the agency tracking the developments and enquiring about their chances every once in a while.

The waiting period is responsible for many couples registering in multiple agencies or looking at options in other states or smaller towns. Arun and Shonali, for instance, got their baby almost immediately after they decided to switch agencies from a well-known Delhi-based institution to Children of the World. Although adoption is becoming an urban trend among couples in their 20s and 30s, adopting older children or children with disabilities is still rare in India. As a result, agencies are seriously hobbled by the number of babies available for adoption compared to the huge queue of couples waiting to be parents.

Of course the process can take even longer for non-resident parents. As Eron and Pritha found out, it may take significantly longer for the baby to first move into foster care and then complete the legalities and be eligible to travel abroad. Inter-country adoptions also require the parents to go through one of the CARA-approved agencies in their country of origin/residence and that process can and often is both time-consuming and costly.

Registering in Multiple Agencies

CARA's public information officer Dr Jagannath Pati says that typically parents are advised to register with a single agency rather than hedging their bets with multiple agencies. But till recently that never stopped parents from hedging their bets with multiple registrations. Arun and Shonali, for instance, signed up with as many as six agencies, after checking the list on the CARA website. This in the end stood them in good stead when they had 'issues' with the agency of their first choice. They went to the others they had registered with and finally settled for Children of the World, from where they got their baby in a matter of less than a month. They were told that a two-year-old registration was perfectly valid and that they were lucky that a baby was available at the precise time they came calling. CARA's new guidelines say home study reports too will remain valid for two years but the parents' medical history should not be more than a year old.

Earlier there was no rule that forbade prospective adoptive parents from registering with multiple agencies and in fact many did. As discussed earlier, the rules have now changed. With prospective parents far outnumbering the babies up for adoption, the queue is often long as is the wait. There is also no rule that says you cannot register with an agency in another state or town. As CARA clarifies, if you're from Bangalore and want to sign up with an agency in Delhi, you are free to do so.

'But you will need to contact the Adoption Coordinating Agency of a particular city or state for further details.'

The choice of agency and familiarity with the adoption regulations are all small steps towards your final goal of becoming parents from the heart. But they are important steps. The more well versed you are with what is expected of you, the less likely you will be to suffer any unpleasant surprises. Being well informed is the first step towards being in control of what is still, despite the new guidelines, a lengthy legal process to parenthood.

2

The Process

In the months that followed after they'd registered themselves, I would often chat with Shonali about the proverbial butterflies in the stomach. She and her husband Arun had gone through a traumatic time trying to conceive but each time, she miscarried at different stages of the pregnancy. Her medical condition baffled and depressed Shonali. She told me it felt like there was something wrong with their hard disk even though there was no malfunctioning part in either of them. Once they signed up for a baby though, the couple decided to ready themselves for the parenting job. They bought a lot of parenting books, routinely chatted with their parents for tips and waited for the agency to get back. During that period, Shonali would often ask me, 'We've chosen the agency and registered ourselves...now what?' For couples who have waited a long time and battled medical problems to become parents, the wait for the baby can seem never-ending. I remember we spent some anxious moments when the agency did not get back for six months after we registered. We spent our time working on a Plan B or C and setting an outside time limit after which we would register in agencies in other cities. But beyond that, the time waiting for a baby can be well spent preparing for the baby's arrival and getting ready to go through the process of adoption.

Home Study Visit and Getting to Know the Baby

One of the questions that was on top of our minds in those weeks and months was 'how should we prepare for the social worker's visit?' We had no idea what the criteria for eligibility were and whether what we said and how we said it would impact our chances of getting our baby. We were understandably nervous because we were working, till then, in a bubble. Apart from our immediate family no one knew we were going in for adoption. In hindsight, that wasn't such a great idea and when we opened up and started seeking advice and opinion on what to do if the wait for the baby turned too long, we came across practical advice on how to deal with the entire process of adoption from home study to facing the magistrate to getting the baby's birth certificate out for her passport.

The good news is that most of this process is extremely streamlined and the agency does a good job of informing the parents on the steps ahead. For instance, when we got a call from our agency nearly six months after registering, we were told that there was a baby for us and we needed to clear the home study report before we would be allowed to see our baby. The social worker who visited us was very genial and she did not make us feel intimidated in any way. Yet, we felt far more confident facing the home study after we spoke to some of the other adoptive parents in our circle of friends. Essentially the only critical question we faced during the home study was the question of disclosure. That and repeated queries about whether the extended family—grandparents, uncles, and aunts—was on board were the recurrent themes during the home study interview.

Later, while researching for this book I found out that there have been instances when a couple has been rejected because the in-laws did not seem totally keen on the idea of adoption. Indeed, some agencies actually include a no objection certificate from the grandparents as part of the necessary paperwork though it is NOT mandated by law. If you are living with parents and in-laws or extended family, you will need to get them on board very early so that the baby gets nothing short of a heartfelt welcome in her new home. Indeed, adoption expert Vinita Bhargava says she actually spoke to each and every member of her family individually to explain their decision to adopt, before her daughter came home. She says she faced mostly curiosity, not resistance, which is understandable since adoption was not a very common trend a couple of decades ago and the decision to adopt when she already had a biological child must have baffled many.

The tone and depth of the home study will depend upon the social worker and the agency. In Shonali and Arun's case, for instance, the social workers did a thorough inspection of their background and the rapport that husband and wife share. 'We were asked stuff like say ten nice things about each other and ten not-so-nice things as well,' remembers Shonali. It was almost like a game and she couldn't stop herself from giggling. 'I guess they wanted to see whether our marriage was strong and our relationship really healthy,' she says. The social worker also asked detailed questions about the couple—background, schooling, college education, how they met, where they met, whether it was a love marriage or an arranged one, relationship with parents, relationship with in-laws, details about immediate family including brother, sister-in-law, salary, investments, property details...in short the whole nine yards. The detailed—three-hour-long—visit impressed Shonali and Arun because they realized that the agency wanted the best for the baby and needed this information to ensure the baby went to the best home possible. The social worker also asked them about the role of parents and quizzed the couple on how they planned to tell the world that their daughter is adopted. That's a little different from what we were asked—how do you explain to your child that she's not born from your tummy—but in effect it is meant to give the agency an idea of whether the parents are confident about their decision and comfortable with the concept of adoption.

The home study interview has now become a lot more streamlined thanks to the newly announced adoption guidelines from CARA. The guidelines clearly chalk out what the social worker should look out for in a home study. 'It is important to know the couple's general attitude towards adoption particularly of an unrelated child and the motivating force behind their decision to adopt,' say the new CARA rules. The idea is to weed out parents looking to fulfil some kind of emotional or psychological void through adoption. That would include looking for a replacement for a child who has died, looking for a playmate for a biological child, or even looking for an emotional anchor for a parent or grandparent who may be ailing or depressed. In short, the home study report will try to gauge if the prospective parent is looking for a child to plug a gap in her personal life. 'Motives that focus on the needs of the child rather than those of the adoptive parents are acceptable,' says the rulebook. The home study report will also try and gauge the couple's attitude towards illegitimacy—given that many children up for adoption are born to unwed mothers—and most importantly will explore 'whether both the spouses are equally eager to adopt or if one of them is going along with the plan just to please his or her partner.'

Along with age, financial details, number of years of marriage, the report also has specific sections devoted to 'attitude of grandparents', 'details of other children and family members including extended family', relationship between husband and wife and a detailed 'psychosocial assessment'. The latter includes emotional health, value system, social status, quality of marital relationship, and previous history of divorce or live-in relationship. The last factor, say adoption experts, could be troublesome. That means if you're in a live-in relationship, not only will you not qualify for a child till you get married, but your earlier status may influence your chances even afterwards.

CARA's new guidelines also suggest that the social worker will counsel the parents before the home study report to create awareness about the entire process of adoption. During the counselling sessions, the social worker, says the rulebook, will concentrate on the following:

1. Emotional readiness of couples aspiring to adopt;
2. Acceptance of adoption as an alternative way of building a family;
3. Parenting and disciplining;
4. Sharing the facts of adoption with the child;
5. Child's need for search of roots;
6. Bonding and attachment with a child not biologically related;
7. Concerns about the child's social background and genetic factors;
8. Issue of selecting the child; and
9. Any other issue that might emerge.

That's also when the prospective adoptive parents will be asked to touch base with various adoptive parents' associations and other adoptive families to get a better idea of what to expect (this aspect is dealt with in greater detail in Chapter 7: Networking).

Aside from official guidelines, explaining your decision to close family and friends is important because these are relationships for a lifetime and how they react to and adapt to the baby will have a lasting emotional impact. In Radhika and Sumit Bawa's case, their daughter Trisha* went through considerable emotional turmoil, part of which was exacerbated by the fact that her patrician paternal grandparents did not accept her till her late teens. It took years of emotional investment on the child's part before the grandparents finally came around. But it took a toll on Trisha.

Sometimes even initial apprehension can make way for complete adulation once the grandparents actually see the child. In Shonali's case, for instance, her father did have some apprehensions but when he saw his granddaughter he was so sold on her that he would not let anyone else even touch her. 'He spends all his time playing with her and making faces for her,' says Shonali. And just like Kiki resembles my mother, Shonali's baby looks a lot like her grandfather. 'Every time someone says she looks just like him, my dad puffs up with pride,' says Shonali.

In our case while both sides of the family—my mother, mother-in-law, brother, sister-in-law, grown-up nephew and niece—were immediately on board, there were some questions from our circle of acquaintances and friends.

I still remember one friend asking me what prompted us to go in for adoption since we were so completely comfortable being a DINK couple for so long and I have never, by my own admission, been much of a baby person, preferring dogs instead. My answer that pets are babies too and they offer the most comprehensive parenting course with practical experience one can get anywhere and short of actually parenting a child they are the next best thing seemed to pass muster. I also explained that there's a time for everything and we felt we were now ready to become parents. We weren't earlier. Simple. That explanation is something pet-loving parents like Probir and Madhumita wholly endorse. Madhumita who has always had dogs in her family and was incredibly depressed when her pet pooch passed away, managed to get over her blues when Preeti* came home just months later. 'I think of it as a new window opening up after a door shut in my face,' says Madhumita. 'Growing up with pets has made me very child friendly from a young age...I love babies and I love dogs and there's really little difference between the two.'

Involving friends and family in the entire process can make baby's homecoming truly memorable. Shonali and Arun were accompanied by his parents when they went to the agency to bring their daughter home. Her parents waited at home. Later, when the extended family saw the baby for the first time, Shonali's favourite uncle made a beautiful remark. He said, '*Yeh sab kismet ki baat hai...is bachchi ki kismet hamari family se juri hui thi...*' In Jayanti and Pronnoy's case, baby Torsha* was first taken to a Kali temple and then a Durga temple before going home. 'Our friends supported all the way—the first guest brought a silver rattle and another walked in with a packet of stuff for the baby...she was accepted and welcomed by everyone,' remembers Jayanti.

For parents their earliest and most precious memory of their child is their first glimpse of her. Our first glimpse of our baby was a deeply emotional experience particularly when my husband held out his finger and a still sleeping Kiki, wrapped in layers of pink swaddle cloth, instinctively grabbed it. It was love at first sight. We felt she was meant to be our child as we were meant to be her parents. It seemed almost preordained. After that 'first day, first show', we visited the agency several times during the week before Kiki came home. I learnt to hold her and help her be comfortable in my arms—I had never before held such a small baby ever—and to interpret her various cry tones as hungry, wet, sleepy etc.... though it would still take her several weeks before she became used to my smell and face.

Getting acquainted with the baby is a really good idea because it helps reduce the infant's initial stress of grappling with an entirely new ecosystem including new sights, sounds, and smells. As the baby transitions from the agency nursery to her home, she will miss her favourite caregiver, miss the way she was held or fed or the smell of her bed linen or even the bawls of the babies in the cot next to hers. Kiki, for instance, took well over a month and a half before she settled in and felt comfortable in her new surroundings. Other children may take longer or less depending upon their attachment to their caregiver at the agency. But if the baby is supposed to travel once the formalities are through—as in the case of intra-country adoptions—it is a particularly good idea to spend as much time as possible with the baby so that she gets acclimatized to her parents at least. That way she will have her parents' familiar faces around when she transitions to her home in a new country.

Baby Lily for instance settled in beautifully when her parents Eron and Pritha took her home after protracted head-butting with the adoption lawyer. The long-drawn-out process was complicated by the fact that Eron is a British national who was working in India when he registered for adoption and was now posted in the US. And his wife Pritha is an Indian national. However, Pritha spent the entire six-odd months visiting her baby every day at the agency and spending time with her. So by the time Lily came home, she had started to bond well with her mother and had no problems settling in, either at her grandparents' house in Delhi or when she finally flew home to the US.

Most excited parents take pictures of the first time they see their baby...it is an incredibly beautiful and emotional moment. For the parents it's a combination of wish fulfillment and anxiety about the parenting responsibilities that lie ahead. Yet nine out of ten parents we spoke to preferred to wait at least a couple of months before sharing baby's first photographs with the wider world. Shonali, a regular on Facebook, did not post anything that would give the wider world a clue about her impending motherhood. Indeed when she did inform me, it was a private mail and she has just posted pictures of her baby, a good six months on. 'I am just a little bit superstitious about these things,' she says and I completely understand. We had rushed in and mailed pictures of our little angel to pretty much everyone in our wider circle of friends. My mother had warned me against it and I was uncomfortable but my husband, delirious with joy, pooh-poohed the superstition bit. After Kiki fell ill a month later, he agreed he'd been hasty. Part of me tells me this is pure superstition and there's no such thing as 'nazar utarna' but mums are the world's most superstitious creatures. We simply can't risk being otherwise, touch wood.

In Probir and Madhumita's case, they sent out a beautiful message and an accompanying picture of Preeti shortly after the baby came home. And Preeti was none the worse for the wear. So moral of the story—if you feel you want to shout it out from the rooftops, go ahead. If not, keep it quiet and introduce your baby to the world slowly and in tiny installments. But don't forget to document every step of your baby's induction into the family...don't do what adoption expert Lois Ruskai Melina says she did... in the hubbub of travelling home with their newly adopted baby, she and her husband completely forgot to organize a photograph of her at the airport. A stray stranger's Polaroid camera helped preserve that moment for posterity.

Once baby comes home, the first week is a whirl of activity with friends and relatives dropping by to see the baby and the parents running around for medical check-ups, further tests if need be, paperwork, and meetings with the lawyer. Most parents say that though the agency does ensure basic vaccination, it's a good idea to repeat everything. It's also a good idea to repeat the basic tests—HIV, TB, hepatitis, chest X-ray, liver function test, Brainstem Auditory Evoked Responses (BERA) test (for hearing), etc. As Jayanti says, 'No matter what the tests threw up, we would still take our daughter home but I needed to know whether I would have the privilege of seeing her grow from diapers to frocks to saris.'

Apart from the tests, your biggest challenge at this stage will be to choose a good paediatrician, particularly one who will be patient with a neurotic new mum. In Kiki's case, we first opted for a ped our family physician recommended. But he seemed reluctant to take calls at home and over the weekend and fobbed me off the first couple of times saying, 'It's probably nothing...we will monitor it and maybe take a look at it on Monday.' Mind you I wasn't acquainted with baby's habits at that point—didn't know that she already had a runny tummy which was acting up more on account of her transition stress. I felt idiotic... it made me feel I had no one to turn to. After a week I changed the ped—the new doctor, the genial, elderly 'Doctor Dadu' whom Kiki grew to love, was comforting, confident, and ready to hand-hold even in times of imagined crises. He was a lifesaver, in more ways than one.

The Legal Process

Typically, the entire legal process of getting the adoption order and the birth certificate out takes anywhere between four and six months. I remember, we took Kiki home end February, our first appearance before the magistrate happened in May, and we got the adoption order by September. The birth certificate took another month or so and we had Kiki's passport ready 18 months after she came home. In baby Lily's case, the process of getting the relevant papers and passport took an additional four months on account of the legal complications arising out of multiple nationalities and country of work.

The process also differs from agency to agency...in our case the sisters at Missionaries of Charity asked us to complete the paperwork only when they found our baby and just before the home study. In Shonali and Arun's case, the agency demanded the entire list of documents at the time of registration. That's because the couple had registered nearly two years ago and were revisiting the agency after a fruitless search with another agency. CARA's new guidelines, though, lay out the time map clearly enough. Under the new rules, the agency will need to get the home study report done within a maximum of two months after registration. The parents in turn will need to confirm their acceptance of the child shown to them within ten days. And once the 'referral' is accepted, the agency has to file for legal proceedings within ten days. That takes care of the kind of hassle that Shonali and Arun faced when their lawyer, for whom this pro bono work was clearly low priority, delayed the court procedure and refused to even entertain calls from the couple.

For in-country adoption, parents will register with only one agency online. For inter-country adoption, parents will register with the Authorised Foreign Adoption Agency (AFAA) or the central authority in their country of residence. In case there is neither, non-resident Indians may approach the Indian high commission or embassy to process their papers and forward their case to CARA.

Once they register (complete with the necessary documents, discussed in detail in Chapter 1: The Decision), the agency will hand out a registration slip. The agency will then conduct counselling sessions to prepare parents for the special challenges of adoptive parenting followed by the home study report, discussed in greater detail earlier. The home study report is valid for up to two years in any part of the country and the medical examination report of the parents is valid for one year. After this, the parents will be shown a maximum of three children for a possible match. If the parents is decide to adopt one of the three 'referrals', they will need to send in a formal acceptance letter by signing on the child study report and medical examination report of the child within a period of ten days. The new rules offer parents a better idea of the child's health and social background (to the extent available, of course) which was earlier a huge gap that caused parents and children unnecessary anxiety. After this procedure, the parents can sign a foster care affidavit and undertaking before taking the child home under foster care. During foster care, the child can travel within India as long as the parents keep the agency in the loop and are able to produce the child before the court for the final legal process.

The legal process kicks off with the agency filing a petition in the local court to 'obtain necessary adoption orders under the Act within ten days of acceptance of referral' by the parents. The local court, as per the Supreme Court judgment in the case of *L.K. Pandey* v. *Union of India*, will dispose of the case within a maximum period of two months from the date of filing. For the next two years, the agency will conduct half-yearly follow-up visits to check on how well the child is doing.

Once the court proceedings are over and the parents get the adoption deed, they can apply for a birth certificate from the 'competent authority' which means the municipal corporation which governs the area where the adoption agency is located. The CARA rulebook says that the adoptive parents or their attorney can make an application to the birth certificate issuing authority along with a copy of the adoption order and the adoption deed for a birth certificate. The process takes around 21 days to a month and is fairly streamlined. Once you get the birth certificate, you can apply for a passport for the baby.

In the case of foreign nationals living in India, like Eron or Fabrise*, the same rules apply except that when they approach CARA for registration, they should come armed with a no-objection certificate to the adoption from the embassy or mission of the country to which they belong. The rest of the procedure is the same as for in-country adoptions except that the embassy or missions of the country to which the parents belong will give an undertaking to be responsible for post-adoption follow-up checks if the parents relocate after adoption. If not, the agency will conduct the necessary follow ups.

Inter-country Adoptions

Under the new guidelines just released by CARA, all inter-country adoptions will now be routed through the AFAA and CARA itself. These AFAAs are basically foreign agencies that are recognized by CARA. The would-be parents will need to register with the AFAA in their country which will in turn conduct the home study report. Once that's done, the AFAA will prepare a dossier on the prospective parents and send it to CARA (and not to an Indian agency as was the case earlier). CARA will suggest an agency and the AFAA will get in touch with the Indian agency. Once the agency comes back with a possible 'referral' (meaning they indicate they have a child that may fit the expectations of the parents), the AFAA will communicate with the parents and if they okay the 'referral', get back to the Indian agency with 50 percent of the child care corpus which for inter-country adoptions works out to USD 2500 (the total amount to be paid to the child care corpus for inter-country adoptions is USD 5000 under the new rules). The rest of the procedure involves getting a no-objection certificate from CARA which is handled by the Indian agency and once the adoption process and court order in India are in place, the would-be parents need to submit the remaining 50 percent of the child care corpus contribution (worth USD 2500) through the AFAA to the Indian adoption agency. In the case of sibling adoptions, the amount to be paid will be USD 5000 for one child and USD 2500 for 'each of the other child'.

The new rules should iron out some of the problems that overseas parents have in the past faced when adopting from India. In Eron and Pritha's case, they were very unhappy with the services offered by the foreign adoption agency that was affiliated to the Indian adoption agency. The foreign agency tried to make them cough up more (for its own developmental work which had nothing to do with the Indian agency from which they were adopting their baby girl). Also, the foreign agency did not counsel them on the intricacies of the adoption process in India, nor did it prepare them for the legal and other problems they faced. Under the new rules, the AFAA will be responsible for not only counselling would-be parents on the dos and don'ts and rules and regulations concerning adoption in India but also about the customs, traditions, culture, food habits, and other traits which will help them make sense of the child's behaviour. They will also be responsible for organizing get-togethers of Indian adopted kids in that country with help from the Indian embassy or diplomatic mission.

The new rules also take away a lot of discretionary power that adoption agencies earlier enjoyed. While researching for this book I have come across instances of agencies threatening to blacklist a couple and the agency and lawyer jointly intimidating the couple saying that they felt the child–parent match was not suitable because the relationship between the lawyer and the couple had soured. The new rules clearly say the agency has no authority to cancel a match without CARA's say so. If the agency suggests a referral should be annulled, it will need to give reasons why it thinks the parents are not suitable and then CARA will take a final call. This should weed out any bullying antics either by the agencies or the lawyers associated with them. However, to be fair, these instances are extremely rare and in most cases the parents hold the agency and its functionaries in the highest esteem.

Coming back to the timeline, foreign adoptive parents get 45 days to confirm a 'referral' or inform the agency that they're okay with the child shown to them. Since they require a no-objection certificate from CARA, the new rules say this should come within 15 days of applying for it. The Indian adoption agency should file for the court petition within ten days of getting the no-objection certificate from CARA. The court order, including the hearing, should come within two months and the passport within ten days of application. This means the entire process, from green-signalling the referral to taking the child home, should not take more than five to six months at the most.

Once the child goes to her new country, the final legal order for adoption in that country should come within a maximum of two years. If it doesn't, the AFAA will need to inform CARA, the relevant authority or government department in that country, and the Indian diplomatic mission.

The court appearances—typically the parents are expected to show up in court with the child at least once—will also now get streamlined with the coming into force of the new guidelines which clearly map out the timelines for the legal process.

Under the new guidelines, CARA has clearly listed the documents needed for inter-country adoptions. Apart from the home study report which will be handled by the AFAA, parents will need to furnish the following:

1. Recent picture of the would-be parents;
2. Marriage certificate/Divorce decree;
3. Certificate of medical fitness from a doctor;
4. Declaration of financial status of would-be parents with supporting documents, employer's certificate or income tax return order, and bank references;
5. Three reference letters from acquaintances and relatives regarding suitability of the adoptive parents;
6. Adoption decree if the parents have another adopted child from India;
7. Police clearance report;
8. Birth certificate/passport/proof of age, nationality, and citizenship;
9. Undertaking from a relative in the case of single parents;

10. Consent of older child;
11. Apart from this the Indian agency will organize an affidavit and the NOC from CARA.

CARA also clarifies that the home study report in the case of overseas adoptive parents will contain their preference in terms of age of the child, sex, physical or mental condition and location within India. The guidelines also clarify that overseas adoptive parents can take a child in foster care immediately after CARA issues the NOC to the Indian adoption agency. During foster care, the parents cannot take the child out of the city. However, the new guidelines specifically request the courts to dispose of such cases in the 'first hearing itself'.

The new rules, say adoption lawyers, if implemented well, should iron out many of the glitches that earlier plagued the adoption process. Since the guidelines are available online, parents should go through them with a fine-tooth comb. Also any complaints—from stroppy agencies or lawyers acting like they are doing you a favour or even requests for donations—can and should be brought to the notice of CARA. The new guidelines clearly say that any wrongdoing like these will result in the Indian agency being pulled up and it could even lose its accreditation. Remember, no one is doing you a favour here so there's no reason to be beholden to anyone.

Revoking the Adoption

CARA's new guidelines say that for in-country adoptions any disruption before the final court order will result in the agency taking the child back from foster care. If the disruption happens after the court order, then the agency will do whatever necessary, 'including seeking an order in the competent court', to revoke the adoption. In the case of inter-country adoptions, for children taken in under the Guardians and Wards Act 1890 (GAWA 1890), the rules are more complex. If the disruption happens before the child becomes a citizen of his adoptive country, then the foreign agency will withdraw the child, inform CARA and the Indian diplomatic mission, place the child in alternate family care and ask the parents to apply to the Indian court which awarded guardianship to revoke the order, within four months of the child moving out of his adoptive family. If the child is old enough, his decision will be included in the matter. If the child has to be repatriated to India, the AFAA will bear the legal costs in the foreign country and pay USD 5000 which will be handed over to the child when he becomes an adult.

3

Baby Comes Home

IF THE LEGAL paperwork and to-do lists have left you huffing and puffing, take a deep breath. Things will escalate to an entirely different level when you actually bring the baby home. There is the infrastructure to set up and make functional, there are medical issues to deal with, there is the sheer amount of time to devote to the new addition to the family. Add to that the considerable paperwork that needs to be taken care of as the baby passes into foster care and the constant stream of friends and relations who will simply drop by to say hello to baby and you'll have more than enough on your plate.

The biggest problem we faced before baby Kiki came home was the incredibly short notice the agency gave us to get everything in place. In our case, we got less than a week between the home study and bringing baby home, and most of that time was spent taking her to two sets of doctors for some basic medical tests. So rushed were we that we in fact opted out of a series of more detailed medical tests, which would have told us that the baby had a health problem. As it turned out, less than a month after she came home, we had a traumatic medical emergency on our hands.

Emergencies of different kinds can arise in the case of biological babies too, of course, but for adopted infants the level of preparedness on the part of the parents in dealing with them tends to be on the lower side for various reasons. Keeping a few basic things in mind can go a long way in preventing such situations or defusing them more promptly.

Setting up the Home for Baby

I still remember that completely crazy weekend in February when I took time out of my paper's Budget edition preparations to shop for our baby. My husband and I drew up a list and we shared the items in an effort to do things more systematically. But with both my mother and mother-in-law stuck in Kolkata for medical reasons, we had no one to guide our frenzied shopping. Result: when baby came home, we realized we had simply bought the wrong stuff.

First-time parents do tend to go completely overboard while shopping for their baby. With so many brands and such beautiful stuff on display, it's hard not to give in to your temptation to buy pretty frocks, colour-coordinated shoes, princess baby cots, and fancy strollers. Trouble is, a lot of that stuff may look pretty but they can be fairly useless for a small baby. Take baby Preeti's parents Probir and Madhumita. Like us, they got barely a week between their first glimpse of the child and bringing baby home. And like us, they committed some retail faux pas. 'When we went shopping for baby clothes, we picked up stuff that was completely unsuitable—like sweaters with hoods and jumpsuits,' says Madhumita. Making an infant wear complicated clothing like hooded jumpers or rompers is the mother of all bad ideas. Babies don't like being pulled and arm-twisted into fashion wear—in fact they have no sense of either fashion or wear. They burp, spit, barf, and pee constantly so it helps if you choose clothes—frocks, tees, jumpers, pants—that are easy to put on and easy to take off, preferably in instalments. That way if the upper is wet, you can change only that and so on. In other words, tops, tees, sweaters, or frocks should be front open, baggy with simple loop-on buttons, and pants should have drawstrings or elastic bands. Moral of the story: don't go by those cute rompers and squeaky toys—get your basic infrastructure up and running first.

Given how badly first-time parents can go wrong, it's always a good idea to involve friends and family in the preparation process. In Preeti's case, she was saved by Probir and Madhumita's wider circle of friends and family who 'made the whole moment of the baby coming home easy', says Madhumita. One friend sent a cot-load of stuff that her one-year-old had outgrown, including a Jerry mouse stuffed toy. Another brought some handknitted sweaters and a handknitted shawl. Still others brought home crucial paraphernalia like cloth nappies, cot sheets, vests, bibs—'All stuff culled by expert mums who knew what we would need,' remembers Madhumita.

In hindsight, that help is actually crucial. Not only does it make the child feel wanted and special—some of these handmade gifts endure and make for great babyhood stories—they also help prevent boo-boos at your end. For example, we realized, after Kiki came home, that in our enthusiasm to buy pretty things for our child, we missed out on a crucial item of baby infrastructure—a flask. In Shonali's case, it was her mother who came home armed with the humdrum items that first-time parents tend to overlook—two flasks, one for hot water, one for lukewarm, an electric kettle, lots of baby bed sheets, oilcloth, nappies, and a sterilizer!

Buying baby stuff also means you need to check if products meant for cooler climates work in India. For instance, we bought tins of diaper rash cream which simply did not work on our baby. Reason: the cream was too heavy for a muggy and hot climate like ours. Finally I took my mother's advice and switched to coconut oil. Kiki never had a problem with nappy rash again, though the zinc creams sat on our baby shelf for a full year before we threw them out.

Similarly, some baby gels we bought in the UK proved too oily for India. And the princess cot we chose disintegrated after a year, when baby refused to sleep in it. Ditto for a stroller which could be turned into a rocking crib. By the time she was seven months old, and ready to go 'out', Kiki refused to lie down on the cradle stroller and we had to junk it for a lighter version in which she could sit up.

Many of these mistakes are made by biological parents as well. But for adoptive parents, the chances of such bloopers are more likely because we get very little time to get the infrastructure up and running. Biological parents get nine months to prepare themselves and the infrastructure, and the entire extended family chips in, knowing pretty much when the baby is due.

In Kiki's case, we received some excellent help from the ped who gave us a list of basic baby medicines that we needed to keep handy for midnight emergencies. These included a paracetamol, a nasal drop, a colic pain drop, a skin ointment, and something to take care of vomiting. Besides, by the time my mother and mother-in-law came over, Kiki was old enough for us to also try some home remedies like basil leaf and honey for coughs or ginger and honey for nausea.

Having an older or more experienced relative—mother, mother-in-law, or even sister/sister-in-law—around can be the biggest infrastructure support you can arrange before or immediately after baby comes home. But getting good help—either domestic help trained in handling newborn babies or paramedical staff like ayahs recommended by the ped or the hospital to which he is attached—is equally important. If you have no option but to try out a nanny not attached to a medical establishment, you need to do a thorough investigation into just how skilled they are. For instance, we opted for a nanny highly recommended by our friends who assured us that she'd handled newborn babies before. But after Kiki came home, the nanny panicked saying her last assignment involved a pair of toddlers and she didn't really know much about bathing, handling, burping, and cleaning a two month old. We fired her and took our paediatrician's help to appoint someone from the hospital for two months by when I was more confident of handling the baby myself.

Unlike biological mothers, adoptive mothers don't get help from the medical establishment on how to look after the baby once she is born. In *Raising Adopted Children,* Lois Ruskai Melina writes, 'Learning how to care for an infant is built into the process of getting ready for the birth of a baby. Childbirth preparation classes focus not only on breathing techniques during labour, but on how to bathe and feed a baby.' But adoptive parents don't get this buffer and agencies focus on the process of adoption rather than childcare.

That's also why preparing the infrastructure is so crucial for adoptive families. Remember, both the baby and her parents will need to go through a period of major adjustment before they 'take to' each other. And having expert advice or help around can help make sense of some of the muddle.

Though the biggest help can often come from fellow adoptive parents. For instance, Kiki's first couple of days with us was a trying time—she was cranky and battling a slight cold and we were new to parenting, perennially exhausted, and wondering if all this was 'normal'. It was only when we swapped notes with other adoptive parents that we realized the baby was probably used to different sights, sounds, smells in her nursery and the alien surroundings made her antsy, which made us confused and tired in equal measure.

Sometimes adoptive parents, in trying to do things their way, come up with novel solutions that work beautifully. Take Probir, a tech-savvy gizmo geek who turned his daughter's daily routine into an assembly line. There would be bottles lined up, and nappies, toys, wipes, and bed linen—all close enough for the tired parent to reach out and grab whatever they wanted without having to look for them. The assembly line worked particularly well at night, when Daddy had feed duties. The baby's feed times were measured and documented with meticulous precision so that Probir knew exactly when baby Preeti would cry for her feed and where he would find the bottle, water, and formula.

Getting Ready for Baby, Physically and Mentally

Infrastructure is only a small part of getting ready for the baby once you've cleared the adoption process. The much bigger and more critical element is preparing yourself physically and psychologically for the process. Parenting isn't easy. It can be, and often is, mentally and physically extremely taxing. Given that many adoptive parents, like us, are older and therefore physically less agile than those in their twenties, the physical strain of parenting isn't anything to sniff away. And yes, unlike biological parents, adoptive parents don't get nine months to prepare themselves for the baby. Typically agencies give anywhere between a week and ten days to complete the formalities and place the child in foster care once the home study and profile match are complete. So be prepared for exhaustion, confusion, a feeling of losing control, fear, anxiety—in short, the whole nine yards.

I still remember how Kiki's first night at home was spent bawling at regular intervals of about one–two hours. I spent the entire night rocking her, giving her feeds, and cleaning her up. Next morning, when my mother called bright and early to check on how I was doing, I was cross, sleep deprived, exhausted, and cranky. My mum chuckled and said, 'You're not the first mother to go without sleep at night. This too shall pass.' My husband's colleagues offered examples of their own kids, many of whom settled into a regular night's rest only in toddlerhood.

The agency told us Kiki was on demand feed and was to be given 3 ounces of formula mixed with tepid water every three hours. Yet when she came home, she seemed to require more than that and I wasn't sure if increasing her feed so quickly would upset her digestion. Adoptive babies often are hungrier than usual, not because the agency does not look after them well, but because a sense of security and undivided parental attention improves their appetite. Shonali and Arun, for instance, saw their three-month-old baby demanding more frequent feeds almost immediately. 'She's one hungry baby,' says Shonali, wondering, like me, how frequently she should up the amount of feed. That's also what Probir and Madhumita experienced with baby Preeti. 'She used to be desperately hungry all the time and would often hold on to the bottle with a look that seemed to say, "THIS IS MINE AND NO ONE CAN TAKE IT AWAY FROM ME!"' says Madhumita.

In our case, Kiki's improved appetite coincided with some colic pain and loose motions so I had to actually slow down the tempo and gradually increase both the quantity and timings of the feed. Getting the temperature right was another hiccup—it took us a couple of days to figure out just how tepid the baby wanted her milk to be. We also tried, desperately and unsuccessfully, to change baby's sleep timings. The first month at home, Kiki would stay up the entire night and go off to sleep in the morning. Advice from parents and parents-in-law encouraged us to get her to stay up in the daytime so she would sleep at night. It didn't work. Why? Because adopted children take a while to get used to their surroundings enough to change their institutional habits. Till they get acclimatized to their new home, they tend to cling to the routine they were used to. Eventually Kiki did change her sleep cycle. By the time she was five months old, she would sleep soundly through the night and wake up at six-thirty in the morning.

While going through those first couple of days of adjustment, I would often be wracked by guilt. I would wonder if the baby was crying because I didn't know how to hold her or wasn't doing something right. I was convinced I didn't qualify for the job and so was doing it badly. Parenting is the only job for which you don't have to take a test and flash a degree. But after a decade and a half of reporting and newsroom antics, I was convinced I wasn't passing muster.

To be honest I did make many mistakes, some of them grave. For instance, I accidentally nicked baby's cuticles while trying to clip her nail when she was five months old. And I think I allowed her to be taken to the park a wee bit early—at three months. I have also given her a way higher dosage of paracetamol when she had a slight fever because I took the instructions from the paediatrician on the phone. That last boo-boo scared me so much—we spent the entire night sitting up and watching her breathing—that I decided I would not take any instructions on the phone till I was confident of and attuned to her medical routine. Within a year, though, I was so used to what the doctor prescribed for basic problems—cough, cold, fever, tummy ache, loose motions, skin rash—that I would often give her a dose and then check with the doctor later who would simply say, 'You know what to give her. Try that, if she doesn't improve call me back.'

Adoptive parents do tend to go a little overboard with precautions. In a way it's necessary because adopted children are often underweight and deprived of that biggest nutrient and immunity builder—breast milk. Also they take a while to get used to the new surroundings and sometimes even different temperatures and climate. Take baby Lily, Eron and Pritha Vaughn's little girl. A sunny child, she quickly adapted to her new environs except in one respect. In the agency nursery, she had been confined almost entirely indoors so when she came home and was taken out to the garden, she was completely 'blinded' by the bright Delhi sun! It took her a while to get used to the idea of a sunny outdoors but when she did, the next step—getting used to a cold and snowy Washington DC when the couple moved—was much easier. In fact, she simply loved the snow.

Shonali on her part decided she would wait for a while before giving the baby her first bath at home. 'I am not a very baby person,' she says. 'So I was really scared. I didn't know what temperature would be right for her.' This kind of dilemma, even in the smallest of actions, is typical of adoptive parenting. You simply don't know enough (a) about parenting and (b) about the infant's earlier circumstances. So both baby and parents take a while to get used to each other.

Psychologically, the sudden arrival of the baby can and does have an unsettling impact. Like me, Shonali, an independent, career-oriented person, had to grapple with the loss of personal freedom and choice once baby came home. In the first couple of months, the mother in particular is completely homebound—no gymming, no coffee with gal pals, no work, not even some me-time in the form of a favourite telly show or a book read. It can leave you exhausted, cranky, and guilty—all at the same time. What helps is if the couple make this a way to bond. In Probir and Madhumita's case, that's how it turned out. 'It was all a first for us—potty, pee, crying ill health…' Madhumita remembers, but with a hands-on husband who wanted to be a part of the entire process, never once grudging the loss of sleep or the exhaustion, it became a great joint effort.

In the process, the couple discovered their own means to handle Preeti—their first baby steps in parenting as it were. Probir got a baby alarm and Preeti would sleep when he turned it on. That, plus her favourite Jerry mouse toy, gave the tired couple the occasional nights of undisturbed sleep. In Kiki's case a favourite pillow and a stuffed toy—christened Woofus the Bow Wow—did the trick and soon we realized it wasn't difficult to get baby to sleep at the same time that we did. Similarly her tech-savvy brother-in-law got Shonali a baby monitor with night vision cameras that he connected to their laptop. That way, once baby went to sleep in the bedroom, the couple could take a break and watch a film or TV show in the drawing room with one eye on the monitor to check if the baby was lying on her back and if everything was okay.

Medical Records and Tests

One of the biggest complaints that adoptive parents have—and that includes us—is that the current rules in India do not make it mandatory for the agency to disclose the biological mother's medical record. This can be a huge problem if the baby gets some infection that is dormant and does not show up in clinical examination, not to mention genetic and other disorders. Adoptive parents are typically given a basic health chart by the agency which includes HIV, TB, and a couple of other tests, along with birth weight and basic vaccines given at birth. But there's no way of finding out, for example, if the birth mother or the extended biological family have any genetic disorders, psychological problems, inherited diseases like diabetes, asthma, or even a history of cancer. This is a huge lacuna in the process that can come up throughout the child's lifetime as medical bolts from the blue.

Most adoptive parents face some form of medical scare—some not serious, others full blown. In our case, just a month after baby came home, she suddenly developed a form of virulent, raging pneumonia that required her to be put into neonatal ICU. The doctors tried a number of antibiotic families and wanted to know if the biological mother had TB or suffered a history of drug resistance. We had no clue. In the end, the treatment progressed through trial and error because we simply did not know whether the infection came from one of the caregivers at the agency or from the biological mother. In effect, the paediatrician and his team had to function with a medical blindfold.

That's why it is very important to do an extensive series of tests before the baby comes home. Many parents don't get into that because they are rushed for time and feel it's tantamount to some kind of screening process. In reality it's necessary because that way you'll be prepared for any medical emergency that may come along. If you know the baby already has some congestion in the chest, the doctor can start the treatment immediately and you won't need to wait till it blows up into an emergency.

Take Preeti, Probir and Madhumita's little girl. The test report that the agency handed out simply did not 'look right'. The couple consulted a paediatrician of their choice who did all the tests—including TB and HIV—and got all the vaccine shots all over again. Like us the couple first went to a ped recommended by the agency but were not happy with his very basic clinical examination. Referring the baby to another ped threw up some potential hearing problems. The doctor suggested a BERA test to check if the problem was serious. The result was positive and the couple then spent the next several weeks going to a number of functional specialists, none of whom gave any conclusive diagnosis. It was only when they took the child to their family physician that the possibility of something as simple as ear wax came up. In the end it turned out to be wax but the anxiety derailed the couple's personal celebration. In hindsight, Madhumita says that the agency's fact file and the referred doctor's medical certificate were both useless. In our case, we were hobbled for choice since the agency does not allow would-be parents to take the baby to a doctor too far away. Being Gurgaon residents, the doctors we trusted were too far from the agency for us to take the baby to them for a check-up.

Coming back to the medical angle, it's a good starting point to repeat all the tests, particularly TB, HIV, Hepatitis B, BERA hearing tests, eyesight and neurological tests, chest X-ray, a liver function test, and anything else the doctor may suggest. In Shonali and Arun's case, the first baby they were offered had a congenital CMV infection for which the doctor suggested a torch test. Also, even if the baby is very small when she comes home, the agency gives a set of basic vaccines like BCG and polio drops. But it is always a good idea to repeat all vaccines. That way the parents know for sure what the baby has been vaccinated against and are prepared for any emergency. The best option is to quickly find a good paediatrician, preferably someone who has handled adopted kids before, and get him on board immediately. Once the ped takes over he can then make allowances for the gaps in baby's medical history and treat her accordingly.

At any rate it's always a good idea to get an opinion other than from the ped referred by the agency. In most cases, the medical examination is a proforma routine procedure and if you want more details you need to get an independent opinion. Eron and Pritha, for instance, took their baby for a thorough check-up to the Apollo Hospital instead of the clinic suggested by the agency.

The biggest worry that adoptive parents nurse is the fear of the unknown. Take Jayanti whose biggest fear after her adopted daughter came home was of losing her. 'Doctors said these children come from deprived backgrounds so a lot of diseases are likely, including TB, HIV, schizophrenia, and my biggest fear was "Will I lose my baby?"' remembers Jayanti. Like Madhumita, she too feels some degree of disclosure from the agency is critical and can save a lot of trauma both for the child as well as the parents.

Of course even the basic medical information that some agencies offer is way more than what is available in the case of abandoned babies. Children adopted from 'homes' or found abandoned in public places come with zero medical history. The adoptive parents won't even know if the birth was normal or a Caesarean birth. They will have no means of finding out if the birth mother had any medical problems and what kind of infections the baby may have faced till she was adopted. Even the birth weight, in those cases, is unknown and if your baby's circumstances are similar to that, it's best to keep the ped in the loop from day one and let her take the baby's treatment and care forward, including the diet chart and vaccine schedule.

Paediatricians say most birth defects occur due to rubella or German measles, CMV, syphilis, encephalitis, parvo virus, and sometimes chickenpox. In obvious cases like Down's syndrome, the defect shows up early enough for the doctors to be able to diagnose it. In some cases, such as metabolic imbalances, the baby may not 'look' in any way different but again a trained ped will be able to take a call. What the peds can't track till the child is old enough to show behavioural changes are psychological problems and then too they may mimic teenage tantrums.

Battling Institutional Care

Most adopted babies are underweight. Partly because the mother may have faced some health or nutritional problems during pregnancy and partly because institutional care, no matter how good, can never substitute for the kind of single-minded attention the baby gets at home from her parents. When Kiki came home at two and a half months, she was tiny—weighing just under 3 kg. It took us around four months to get her to plump up.

Eron and Pritha had a similar experience. When baby Lily came home, she was really scrawny. But three months of concerted care later, she turned into a 'Sumo wrestler'. The best thing to do is to trust the ped with the food chart and slowly increase feed times and quantities. Of course, if you've adopted a slightly older child, the weight gain may be slower because the baby takes longer to get over the undernutrition in the initial months. For example, though perfectly healthy, baby Preeti was never as chubby as Kiki became in her infancy and it took her parents some focused effort—including strict adherence to a diet chart—before she started gaining weight and hit the 'normal' weight range. Meanwhile her parents went through some tense moments particularly when her teething was also delayed. It took a jocular remark by the paediatrician—'Have you ever seen a toothless toddler?'—to finally put them at ease. Later they realized it was more of a genetic trait rather than a health issue.

Adoptive parents need to be extremely patient with their child's growth chart. The weight gain may not be rapid. The general growth may be slow. But as long as the baby's metabolism is all right, there shouldn't be anything to worry about. Rushing it could cause tummy upsets and colic pain at best—something that we faced with Kiki—and liver problems at worst. Also, many adopted kids—like their biological counterparts—are born with some kind of jaundice and in the absence of breast milk, getting them to come up to scratch isn't easy. Typically, very small infants can shake off their institutional routine within a month or two and quickly gain weight. With older babies, that schedule is longer though they too eventually shake off their institutional baggage. My experience is that introducing solids early on is a really good idea because (a) it relieves colic pain and other tummy problems; (b) it substitutes the nutrition that the baby misses out on by not breastfeeding. I introduced solids the day Kiki turned four months old and her weight gain happened immediately afterwards.

Maternity/Paternity Leave

Can adoptive parents expect maternity or paternity leave? Our experience as well as that of a number of adoptive parents in our wider circle of friends convinced us that this issue is typically handled by different employers on a case-by-case basis. Government employees are entitled to 135 days of leave if they adopt a baby 'upto one year of age', as per a Government of India memorandum dated March 31, 2006. According to this notification, adoptive mothers with 'fewer than two surviving children' will get 135 days of child adoption leave for adopting a baby of up to one year of age.The memorandum also says that 'the maximum period of one year leave of the kind due and admissible (including leave not due and commuted leave upto 60 days without production of medical certificate) will be reduced by the age of the child on the date of adoption without taking into account Child Adoption Leave'. Which means if the child is two months old at the time of adoption, the mother can claim up to ten months' leave while a six-month-old baby will fetch her mother up to six months leave and so on.

A further update issued in 2009 extended maternity leave for adoptive government servants to 180 days and offered 15-day paternity leave for adoptive fathers 'within a period of six months from the date of adoption'.

Advocate Geeta Luthra says the Maternity Benefit Act (1961) offers umbrella benefits to all mothers but there is still no specific enactment for adoptive mothers in the private sector. 'The government can, if it wants, introduce relevant enactments covering both public and private sector, as in the case of prevention of sexual harassment in the workplace,' says Luthra. 'But so far, nothing of the kind has been forthcoming.'

As a result, those working in the private sector often need to negotiate for their maternity leave. Some companies have a liberal policy under which parents—both adoptive and biological—get a certain number of days of paid leave. In my case, for instance, my employers were extremely considerate and allowed me the usual three-month leave and some flexi-timing till Kiki was about one year old. But there is no law that mandates maternity or paternity leave for adoptive parents. And the parents are often left at the mercy of their respective HR departments. Many companies do not have a special policy for adoptive mothers and sometimes, when a policy is in place, it is the result of individuals fighting for their rights.

Take the case of Madhumita, baby Preeti's mother. When Preeti came home, Madhumita was working for a reputed consumer durables company with MNC salaries and employment terms. But it had no special policy for adoptive mothers. As a result, Madhumita had to be content with just forty-five days leave—an extremely short time to set up the infrastructure and allow the baby to get acclimatized to her new home. In Shonali's case, her employer, a global IT giant, too did not have a policy till a colleague fought for and got her three-month maternity leave. Moral of the story: the HR policies of private companies are privately driven and don't come under government HR policy. So if your company does not have a policy in place, fight for it. And yes, don't forget to enlist the help of other adoptive parents in your workplace. Madhumita, for instance, is quite clear that though she couldn't fight for her own rights, she would fight for anyone else in her organization who faces the same problem. So don't think you're alone—you never know from where you could suddenly get help.

When it comes to paternity leave, the policy gap is even worse in India. Though an established trend overseas, the concept of paternity leave, even for biological parents, is not common in India. However, here too organizations can and do offer some leave depending on how liberal their HR policy is though nothing concrete is mandated by law. In our case, for instance, my husband got around fifteen days off which proved to be very handy for us. Either way, there's no harm asking for leave and checking with your HR team if it is possible because adoptive parents need to take care of a lot of paperwork and other infrastructure issues, and bonding with the baby happens best when both parents are involved.

In most countries in the West, both maternity and parental/paternity leave for adoptive parents is mandatory. Paternity leave can extend from seven days to much longer, depending upon the country and the length of service. Hopefully, as the number of adoptive parents increase in India, both maternity and paternity leave will become mandatory in our corporate culture as well.

Bonding with the Baby

In the weeks after Kiki came home I would often be wracked by feelings that had little to do with motherly love. The biggest constant was doubt—I would wonder if I, an independent and career-minded person, would ever be able to take to my baby 'like a mother should' and, more importantly, if she would take to me. I still remember that poignant prayer service that the sisters at the Missionaries of Charity (Delhi chapter) conducted for us in their chapel before we took our baby home. They sang some well-loved hymns—both my husband and I, being convent school products, it brought nostalgic tears to our eyes—and prayed that baby Ekta, as she was called in the agency, would be happy with her new parents. For my husband, it was a moment when his whole life flashed before his eyes. He was overwhelmed with emotions and couldn't stop crying. As for me, I was scared stiff. I knew I would now have to look after this cherubic little creature and every action or word from me had the potential to enrich or damage her character. The enormity of it all hit me right between the eyes and left me completely gobsmacked. Oh God, I wondered, how will I ever be a mother. I don't know how.

That feeling of being overwhelmed, of not knowing what to do and how to do things, of always second-guessing my emotions and wondering if I would have felt differently if I were a biological mother are all, I realized, quite normal. In fact, a lot of that jumble of emotions is faced by biological mothers too and not all those feelings are particularly motherly. So if you've just brought your baby home and are going through those same emotions, wondering just when that magic moment of perfect bonding will strike you and your child, relax. It's all part of the parenting experience. And this too shall pass.

When I started sharing my feelings with other adoptive parents as part of researching for this book I was astounded at how many of them admitted to the same emotions. I realized I would have managed my feelings much better had I exchanged notes earlier. Like me, many adoptive mums I spoke to were perennially exhausted the first couple of months of parenting and sometimes felt angry with the baby for being cranky and keeping her awake all night or not allowing her even a minute of me-time. These feelings of anger and frustration are immediately followed by self-doubt. 'Am I a bad mother? Would it be different if my baby was biological?'

The truth is, biological mothers too face many of these emotions but often without the guilt that adoptive mothers burden themselves with. It takes someone like Jayanti, who has both adopted and biological children, to put it all in perspective. Pronnoy and Jayanti's biological son came three years after they adopted their baby girl. A late pregnancy, Jayanti's experience was not quite the stuff of films. In fact she was so unwell that despite breastfeeding the baby, she didn't feel any sense of bonding with him till much later. 'It wasn't a great experience,' she remembers.

'I was tired after the childbirth, ill, exhausted from feeding the baby all night and changing nappies. There was no time to bond.' The bonding happened later, she says, when the baby was big enough for her to cuddle. In fact, she bonded much quicker with her adopted daughter. That experience with biological motherhood convinced Jayanti that the difference between biological and adopted is more in our heads than anywhere else. 'Who says genes come through the blood, they come flying through thin air,' she says.

Of course in many ways the adoptive experience is a little more difficult than the biological one even if one takes into account the pregnancy difficulties. The adoption process can be sudden enough to throw all your plans into disarray. Shonali's first reaction, when the agency told her she could take her baby home was, 'What happens to my pricey gym membership now…shucks, I just paid up.' In hindsight, these small, irrelevant worries seem laughable but when you're in the middle of it all, they seem important enough. In due course though, the bonding kicks in and nothing else matters. For some, the moment is almost akin to baptism by fire. For others, it's less gut-wrenching. In our case, the bonding happened really and truly when our baby was in the ICU battling a galloping pneumonia. When we came back home from the hospital after she was admitted, it hit us that we would now give anything for another sleepless night of baby bawls and hourly feeds. In a sense that crisis made us realize how precious this gift was and we will never forget that lesson in our lifetime.

With baby Preeti and Madhumita too it was ill health that forged a special bond. As she rocked her baby's cradle all by herself while her husband ran around to collect more test reports, Madhumita would often ask Preeti, 'Where's Jerry (her favourite soft toy)?' Every time the baby looked up at Jerry mouse dangling on her crib, Madhumita would utter a soft hurrah—in her heart she knew her baby could hear her voice no matter what the BERA tests said.

Adoptive mums almost always remember their 'moment' when the magic actually kicks in. It can be something as simple as a grin from the baby or something she says when she's older. For Shonali that moment was when her baby rewarded her with a gummy, toothless smile. 'Suddenly it's all worth the while and nothing matters—not the exhaustion, not the lack of privacy, not the total disregard for your personal well-being,' she says.

For me, long after that gut-wrenching moment of truth in the hospital, came my personal reward when Kiki, now a toddler, suddenly gave me a hug one evening and said, 'Mamma, I lub lou.' Can anything beat that feeling?

4

Talking Adoption

I

DISCUSSING ADOPTION IS one of the most critical aspects of adoptive parenting. How to 'talk adoption' is an issue adoptive parents need to figure out from day one, that is, from the would-be adoptive parent stage. Because it is a subject that the social worker may touch upon during the home study visit and your response to how you will explain the adoption story to the child could also determine your eligibility. Indeed Shonali and Arun, after a disappointing run with their first adoption agency, managed to convince the social worker from the second agency they approached, on the basis of their adoption story. 'We told her that it's just a cool thing to do...we think its cool and we'll tell our baby that adoption is cool,' says Shonali. Coming from a hip, upwardly mobile, thirty-something couple, it was the perfect answer.

It isn't easy discussing adoption with a child less than six years old. For one, it's not an easy thing to explain and for another, the child may not even comprehend the real meaning of what she's being told. Single mum Mandira* has tried to explain to her four-year-old, kindergarten-going son Atri* that he is a 'baby from the heart'. Unlike other kids that age, Atri did not dispute that tidbit of information but he has simply decided that all his classmates are adopted too. Mandira was baffled by his comment one day that his classmates Arjun, Shauna, Aryan, Teana, and Meher are *all* adopted. When she asked him why, he said, 'They all wear yellow T-shirts on Tuesdays and Fridays.' Mandira realized that Atri had clubbed all the children in his playgroup as adopted because they all wore T-shirts of the same colour.

Though adoption experts encourage parents to disclose the adoption issue to the child as early as possible—preferably by six or seven years of age—do not be surprised if your preschooler or kindergarten-going child either refuses to discuss adoption, or worse, simply goes into denial mode. Children that age are too small to understand complicated subjects like birth parents and adoptive parents or even couple parents and single parents. So when should adoptive parents initiate the discussion and how often should the parents revisit the topic to make sure the child understands what she's being told?

Most agencies will tell you to start the adoption story when the child is old enough to speak. And that the earlier you start, the better it is. Is it easier to talk adoption with a three-year-old? Absolutely not. We have tried to talk to Kiki about how she came into our lives but, frankly, she seems least interested. With a new school, new friends, picnics, activities, play-outs, and other stuff happening in her life, she really couldn't be bothered about whether she came from Mamma's tummy or her heart. So our job is clearly not even well begun, though we hope when she's a little older, she'll be more willing to listen to the story of how our family came together and Baba and Mamma found their little angel.

Timing of the Talk

Nearly all the parents of infants or toddlers I spoke to while researching for this book maintained that they were not quite sure when to initiate the subject of adoption with their baby. I can speak from experience that it's a tricky question—how do you know if you're initiating the topic too early or too late? I started out by asking

Sister Anthea of Missionaries of Charity (Delhi chapter) and she said you can talk to the kid around the time she's about two-and-a-half or three. In other words, when the child can express herself verbally, it's fine to initiate the topic of adoption.

We decided to do just that, chatting with Kiki about how Baba and Mamma really, really, wanted an angel baby and the sisters helped us get one. But Kiki, who loves stories about her infanthood—including how she was so small that Baba could hold her head on the palm of his hand and rock her to sleep—showed no interest in our adoption discussions. She didn't have a negative reaction but she didn't have a positive one either—she simply ignored the conversation and moved on to something else.

However, our persistence has paid off to some extent. Plus, we have also maintained contact with the agency, hoping that Kiki will accept the sisters and kids at Missionaries of Charity as part of her life and that she will include them in her larger social circle alongside cousins, schoolmates, and neighbourhood friends (see the section Staying in Touch with the Agency below). We believe the references to incidents and routines in her infanthood are becoming clearer as she grows older and we hope in a couple of years she will be ready to hear the full story and understand at least some parts of it.

Many of the parents I spoke to were in favour of introducing the subject as early as possible. From single mums like Rupali Mitra to mixed race couples like Pritha and Eron to mixed (with both adopted and biological children) household parents like Jayanti and Pronnoy, many adoptive parents say it's best to start talking about the issue and using the word adoption as early as possible so the child is aware of the word, if not the meaning and the full connotation. That does not, however, mean that the child will be receptive towards the adoption story—she may, like Kiki, be disinterested. She may, like Lily, be in denial. She may, like Ariana*, pretend the conversation never happened. They may have various reactions to it but at least they will not be gobsmacked when you raise the topic the next time round.

Parents who initiate the adoption discussion early should be prepared to revise and revisit the script several times over till the child is old enough to understand and retain what she's being told. Telling a three-year-old that she's born from the heart and that the sisters gave Baba and Mamma their angel baby is pretty much like narrating a favourite fairy tale—the child will forget the story and what it tries to convey sooner than you can mutter Cinderella! Parents need to build fun activities around the theme and revisit the story reasonably often over the next couple of years till the child is old enough to remember and understand.

However, it is really not a great idea to leave the disclosure till very late because the older the child the more traumatic the reaction. Middle schoolers (between nine and twelve years of age), for instance, are intense conformists—that's the time when the question of family and fitting in crop up and the children find it very difficult to reconcile their 'difference' with their desire to fit in.

Tips and Tools

Every parent has their own way of broaching the concept of adoption with their child. All of them are effective in their own way and parents devise small, practical things as they go along to make adoption a word in the child's world. What I shall be putting down here are some such examples but that doesn't mean you can't have your own activity or tool with which to explain stuff to your child. All of these ideas work to make the child comfortable with the word adoption and make the whole subject fun so that they don't grow up considering it to be a taboo of some sort, or thinking of it as a subject that made them unhappy and anxious.

Our experience as adoptive parents has convinced us that it is probably better to initiate the adoption story through activities rather than try explaining things to a toddler or a preschooler. On our part, our biggest adoption tool and one that we have spent—and will spend—many happy hours putting together is the baby book. Every baby has a baby book—it's invariably one of the gifts that come along when a newborn comes home. But for the adopted child the baby book is both a souvenir and a way of rooting her firmly in her family. The pictures and memory minders—from air tickets to toffee wrappers—should help her understand she has a shared past with her parents and her immediate family, as indeed she will have a shared future with them.

We've kept lots of pictures of everything—from the first time Kiki ate at the dining table to her first scribble and all the ceremonies she participated in as a baby from the mukhebhaat or first-taste-of-rice ceremony (the most important one for the baby in a Bengali household, akin to the mundan ceremony popular down south), to the first Durga Puja, the first Diwali, Holi, Bhaiya Duj, and Christmas. Every vacation, every visit to her grandparents, both maternal and paternal, every new dress she wore, every outing has been photographed and recorded in the baby book. It has pictures of her favourite toys, first friends, first ice cream, first trip to the mall, first bath, first school work at her playschool, first fancy dress party, first time she met my mother's pets—in short, there's nothing, important or trivial, that we have left out.

Kiki loves to leaf through the book and point out to her friends or their parents just how tiny she was. She giggles when she sees pictures of her taking a bath and wonders why she's looking so grumpy even though everyone was making such a fuss over her on her mukhebhaat day and first birthday. Unlike other baby books, we have not used ours to track Kiki's first tooth or her medical chart. This book is not a baby report card, it's a fun activity for us to share with our baby as she grows up and wants to know what she was like when she was a chotto baby. In time we hope we can use it to explain our adoption story better.

Apart from the baby book we have also tried to start talking to Kiki about how our family came together. We have tried to keep it simple and straightforward. Our story goes something like this: 'Baba and Mamma wanted a little angel baby to love and play with. So we went to the sisters at Missionaries of Charity and they helped us to find you. You were destined to fill up our lives with happiness and the sisters helped bring us together.'

I must confess we haven't made much headway with the story—Kiki is simply not interested. She'd much rather listen to how Mamma would burp her as a baby and how she would cry and Mamma would give her milk and rock her to sleep. She even mimics those same activities with her favourite doll, feeding, burping, and rocking her to sleep.

Others like Madhumita and Probir use the night-time prayer to prepare their baby Preeti for the adoption discussion. 'We have already started in a small way,' says Madhumita. 'Every night, before going to bed, we say a small prayer. It's a simple prayer thanking God for everything.' The couple feel that they can later slowly introduce the adoption story and tell Preeti that she came into their lives because they were meant to be together as parents and child. God brought them together and He wants them to be together—it was all meant to be.

Sohom* and Debjani*, for their part, used the story of Krishna to explain adoption in a positive way. Krishna is a popular myth and associating the story of how their family came together with the traditional tales of parental and filial love that bound Krishna to his adoptive parents Yashoda and Nanda helped give a positive connotation to the adoption discussion. Interestingly, all the Krishna myths centre around Krishna's fondness for his adoptive mother Yashoda. Popular art or culture has little reference to his birth mother Devaki. Even the Krishna hymns talk about Yashomati maaiya rather than Devaki.

This is, in fact, a tool recommended by many agencies to parents—recounting of stories from Indian mythology, especially the Krishna legend, that make the adoption issue clear to the child without hammering home the point. Following the recommendation of the sisters at Missionaries of Charity, we bought a CD of the animated film *Krishna*. Kiki loves watching it. She may not understand the adoption theme in the story right now but hopefully when we explain it to her a couple of years later, we will be able to use the Krishna legend as a reference point.

Still others like Rupali Mitra used images from popular culture to explain the concept to their child. Rupali remembers that she used a water filter ad on TV to initiate the discussion on adoption. Her daughter Ariana would patiently hear her out and then move on to some other subject. As for Eron and Pritha, they have tried to use pictures and books to introduce Lily to the word adoption but she's 'emphatically' not interested.

Staying in Touch with the Agency

Should adoptive parents stay in touch with the agency, to bolster their adoption story? Honestly, like everything else in adoptive parenting, there's no straight answer for this. Though some agencies ask the parents to maintain contact for the next five years and keep sending status reports and pictures, it's really up to the parents to decide. Often it becomes geographically impossible to maintain regular contact with the agency if the family moves out of the city or emigrates.

As parents, my husband and I felt we needed to stay in touch with the sisters at Missionaries of Charity. We have maintained contact with the agency, celebrating two birthdays for Kiki—one for her schoolmates and another with the kids at Missionaries of Charity (there is a 'third' of sorts, with close family, to celebrate the day she came home to us). The idea is to make her comfortable with the physical aspects of the story—the agency, the sisters, the kids, etc.—so that when we use them as references to explain the adoption story, things will be more acceptable to our baby. Because of our frequent trips to Missionaries of Charity, Kiki now recognizes the figures clad in blue-bordered white saris as sisters and associates the reference to the birthday parties we would organize for her there every year—clearly a positive connotation.

When we decided to move from Delhi to Pondicherry, we took the contact number and address of the local branch of Missionaries of Charity so we could continue with our ritual of celebrating two birthday parties for Kiki. So far Kiki has not had a problem enjoying her 'birthday party with the sisters'. For the past three years, she has in fact looked forward to cutting a cake and playing with the kids at the agency. The sisters there still call her Ekta (her name before she came home to us) and have even taken her to the nursery to show her where she used to sleep as a chotto baby. Kiki loves all the extra attention and happily poses with the sisters. But I don't think she associates that yearly trip with anything more than a fun-filled outing. She is simply too young to understand.

Many parents I interviewed while researching for this book have followed a similar routine. Like us, Pronnoy and Jayanti have meticulously maintained contact with their agency Palna and they too celebrate two birthdays for their adopted daughter Torsha. In junior school now, Torsha isn't terribly excited about her Palna birthday parties any more. Kids that age look for other factors in their friends—simply being of the same age group is not enough for them to bond. The Palna kids are not from her school, they don't share her taste in music or films or all the fun things she does with her friends. So she finds it difficult to think of them as friends. Her kid brother, on the other hand, is still young enough to enjoy all the fuss that a birthday party entails and routinely complains why he too can't have a Palna birthday party like Didi. Indeed it is his enthusiasm that has kept the tradition alive in their household.

Adoption experts say it is not uncommon for kids to reject these traditions only to come back to them later in life. Children in teenage years may go through an identity crisis and an intense desire to conform to their peer group. So, if no one else has two birthday parties, a teenager could feel embarrassed to admit she does. Teen- and tween-agers may also reject other adoption-related celebrations, such as the day they came home, because at that age the children may still be sorting out their emotions about their birth parents. By the time they are in their twenties, these issues normally get sorted out in their heads and they look back on these traditions as charming and positive. They may also want to celebrate their identity as the offspring of their adoptive parents and revive the tradition when they have kids of their own.

Staying in touch with the agency can also come in handy when the child grows up and wants to know more about her birth parents. Torsha's parents, for instance, know that at some point she will want to know what her birth mother was like, why she was put up for adoption, and whether she was abandoned or 'handed over' for adoption. 'If Torsha grows up and wants to know more, we will go to Palna and open the files,' says Jayanti. 'If she ever wants to know more about her biological parents I would say to her, "Go to the adoption centre because we don't know. For us it doesn't matter because you are ours."'

That's exactly what Radhika and Sumit Bawa told their now teenage daughter Trisha. When she asked her parents about her biological mum and dad, the Bawas simply told her, 'We don't know. If you want to resolve this, you will have to go to the agency.' The Bawas kept in touch with the agency and mailed them a cheque every year for more than fifteen years. Like us, they maintained an album of photographs and memory minders including Trisha's boarding pass when they brought her home from the agency in Kolkata. When she was eight, the parents took Trisha to the agency to show her the cradle where the caregivers found her. She was interested in the whole process when young but by the time she hit adolescence, she didn't want to go.

Some children, like Eron and Pritha Vaughn's baby Lily, simply don't like the association with the agency from day one. Every time her parents have taken her back to the agency, baby Lily has bawled her heart out. 'Clearly there's some connection there which she does not like and does not want to remember,' says Pritha. Otherwise a sunny and happy child, Lily has made it abundantly clear that she does not want to remember the agency as a reference point in her life.

Some parents, though, feel there's no reason to stay in touch with the agency or to use it as a reference point for the adoption story. Probir and Madhumita are very clear that they don't want to use the agency as a reference point in their adoption discussions. Unlike us, they do not have two separate birthday parties for baby Preeti. They believe they don't need to remind the child where she came from in order to explain to her that she's a baby from the heart. Probir and Madhumita feel it is easier to explain the whole concept of adoption to their child because there's already another adopted child in the immediate family—Preeti's first cousin Pompey. Having two adopted kids, barely three years apart, in the family should not only help the parents talk adoption and make it a word that's used quite often within the family, but also help Preeti process the information and share her grief or turmoil, if any, with a dear sister who also went through the same rite of passage.

Coming Home Stories

It was Bollywood star Sushmita Sen who first used the phrase 'born from the heart' to explain adoption to her daughter. Every parent will have their own 'coming home stories' to explain how Daddy and Mummy 'found their child'. Explaining the difference between biological and adopted to a six- or seven-year-old isn't easy and parents typically use simple, easy-to-understand narratives to drive home the point.

Though the 'you were chosen' story was very common earlier, adoption experts now say it's best not to window-dress the account in that manner. The 'you were chosen' angle actually came from the US. Back in the 1960s, it was common for American adoptive parents to actually go to the agency nursery and pick out their baby. So in a sense, the adoptees were actually 'chosen' and the story was in fact true.

But extrapolating that same story on to a different milieu and time may not work. Agencies don't allow parents to choose babies any more—they do have a couple of options but they don't actually go to the nursery to pick out their baby. Western adoption experts are uncomfortable with the 'you were chosen' theory also because they feel it may make the child feel extra 'special' or 'privileged'—the other extreme of a biased comment that makes her feel in some way 'inadequate'. A sense of entitlement is no more desirable, they say, than a sense of inadequacy. The best way is to say it like it is. The adopted child should know that she's no different—better or worse—than any other child. She's just another 'type' of child in a world that's rich in diversity.

Having said that, I know of many adopted kids who have grown up listening to the 'you were chosen' story and are none the worse for it. In fact Jayanti recounted an amusing incident involving a friend's older adopted child and the biological child. Both teenagers, the two were fighting about using their common laptop and like most sibling squabbles it was a rip-roaring affair. Finally, the brother tried to end the argument saying, 'God, I dunno what made Mom and Dad *choose* you, of all people, to be my sister.' His sister shot back, 'At least in my case they had a choice, in your case they didn't.'

Another easy way to explain the why in adoption is through a story about Daddy and Mummy not being able to have a baby. Many parents I spoke to said their adoption story goes something like this: Daddy and Mummy wanted to have a little angel but could not. So they prayed to God and God asked the agency to help us out. That's how we got you. The only problem with this explanation is that it puts a negative spin on why Daddy and Mummy wanted to adopt baby. If baby grows up thinking it's only because they 'could not' have a child, then a biological sibling later on can create problems.

The adopted child may feel that now that Daddy and Mummy have a baby, they will no longer love her.

My husband and I have started talking to Kiki about how our family came together. We've told her Baba and Mamma wanted to be parents and asked The Divine Mother what to do. The Divine Mother told us to go to the sisters at Missionaries of Charity and they helped us find our little angel. We try not to make it sound like we were sad because we couldn't become parents—the idea is to avoid any negative connotation. We've told her how the first day she met us, Baba held out his little finger and she instinctively grabbed it with her wee hand. We have a picture of this incident so it's fun to chat and leaf through the pictures to tell her how it all happened.

What we have kept at the back of our mind is that we will not:

- Say anything that's not true, including telling her that she was 'chosen', for instance.
- Say anything negative such as that we adopted her because we couldn't become parents any other way. That may make her wonder if we would have had her if we could a biological child.

- Be too adult about it. Some adoption experts advise against using terms like 'babies from the heart' because when the child grows up she will question it as a medical impossibility. That's true but it's a beautiful concept and everything we say need not necessarily be filtered through an adult prism. If as a mother I think it's a good way to explain something to my child, why should I second-guess my instincts?

However, for now Kiki is not interested in knowing about where she came from. What fascinates her are stories of how she was fed, burped, or rocked to sleep and she would mimic these activities with her favourite doll. That does not mean those stories aren't registering somewhere. Kiki routinely surprises us by regurgitating some tidbit from random conversations or stories. For instance, although she showed no interest in the Cinderella story the first time round, she immediately made a connection with the fairy godmother when she came across another fairy caper on TV. The adoption stories too, we believe, are making an impact somewhere and when she's old enough to understand, they will have made her a little bit comfortable with the word adoption.

To go back to the 'babies from the heart' concept, adoption expert Vinita Bhargava, author of the seminal *Adoption in India: Policies and Experiences*, is among those who do not agree with it. She feels it opens up yet another trigger for an 'inquisition'. 'Very soon the child will know that it is medically impossible to be born from the heart,' she says. So if the parent uses that logic to establish a parental bond, it can come unstuck when the child puts everything her parents say under the lens. That can happen in teenage or tweenage years when the peer pressure to conform is highest and the rebellious streak most visible.

All this implies that what you tell the child will also change as you go along and the child learns concepts like being born out of a tummy. Rupali's five-year-old daughter Ariana, though comfortable with and exposed to the word adoption for more than two years now, recently asked her mother if she grew inside her tummy. Around the time they are five to seven years old, children will start asking questions about growing in the tummy and parents need to explain things in a simple, child-friendly manner, particularly if there's a biological child in the household as well.

Jayanti, who has both an adopted and a biological child, says, 'I tell my daughter that a baby can come in two ways—either from the mother's tummy or from the agency.' She feels it's okay to let the child cry and feel grief for a while because that can be cathartic. 'I would tell Torsha, "This is a fact. If it makes you sad, you can cry it out of your system. We are with you and we will help you get over this sorrow."' She goes on to say that it's better for parents to explain why they are telling the child she is adopted. 'I told her, "We chose to tell you the truth because it is a beautiful truth and we're very proud of it. So you should be too." The other option is to lie but if you lie once, you'll have keep lying all your life. And you can't build a life on lies,' says Jayanti.

Jayanti says her story is not so clinical that the child will not be able to relate to it, nor so overly window-dressed that it will send out a patently wrong signal. Jayanti says she tells her daughter that all children are born from the tummy but just giving birth alone does not make people parents. 'Parents become parents through parenting. Who sits by your bedside all night when you are ill? Who brought you up, loved you all the way, cleaned your poo and barf, hugged you when you were sad, and laughed with you when you were happy? Who looks after you all the time, looks forward to your future, and looks back with pride and love on your past? Ma and Baba are not just those who give you birth. They are those who fill your world with love and happiness and look after you forever,' says Jayanti.

Western adoption experts often say that it is important to include the child's biological past in the adoption story even if she was too small to remember anything. For instance, saying that the agency helped Baba and Mamma find baby may make the child grow up thinking she's not woman-born and therefore a freak. As a mother, I find that assumption a bit difficult to swallow. It's important to clarify the role of the birth parents in western society because the law allows the child to stay in touch with his birth parents. Often adoptive parents write directly to the birth mother stating their reasons for adoption and presenting their case as the ideal candidates. That's precisely how Monica and Chandler Bing got their baby in the TV series *Friends*. In India, agencies give no information about birth parents. Sometimes the information may be available, if the child was born at a hospice run by the agency for instance. At other times, the information is just not available. If the child was abandoned in a cradle at the agency or at any other public place, there's no information about her birth parents that even the agency can offer. So the western concept of allowing birth parents a role in the child's ecology doesn't work in India.

Talking about Birth Parents

Having said that, as a parent you will still need to talk about your child's birth parents. Questions about birth parents will crop up in the tween or teen years when the child becomes more conscious of her identity and more confused about it as well. Adoptive parents often agonize over how to describe the birth parents to their child. Is it necessary to find out details about the birth parents so that you can give your child some answers if he or she asks?

In India where records are not nearly as meticulously maintained as in the West, it may be difficult for you to glean information about the child's birth parents. Typically, agencies will maintain a file including some information about the birth parents or at least the birth mother. Some agencies, like Missionaries of Charity, keep records of birth parents, particularly if the birth happened at one of their hospices. But if the child was abandoned, the agency would not have any information to offer either. Sister Anthea of Missionaries of Charity says her agency gives the reasons for adoption and even the mother's name but not the address. 'Now that the records are computerized, it's possible to track cases that happened many years ago,' she says. 'For example, recently a lady called. She's forty and she wanted information about her biological parents.'

Parents like Jayanti and Pronnoy are of the view that the child should be given whatever information is available with the agency. Indeed that's one of the reasons why they have maintained contact with their agency Palna. As a parent she wants to be part of the search if her daughter ever wants to know more about her birth parents. 'We will stand by our child and help her search and we know she will come back to us,' says Jayanti.

Since Torsha is eight years old, the birth parent questions have already started cropping up. For instance, she wanted to know why her birth mother 'gave her up'. Jayanti told her that she must have had some difficulties in raising a child. 'Maybe the biological mother was unwell and could not take care of any baby. Maybe the baby was actually someone else's but came to her by mistake. The baby was meant for us but went to her by mistake so we found our child after she was born to another woman,' says Jayanti.

In Varsha Bhatia's* case the birth parent questions came around the middle school years when the 'concepts of family not connected by blood ties came up. My daughter started asking me, "Would I have been happier had I lived with my birth parents?"' says Varsha. Children that age can conjure up the worst, not knowing anything about their antecedents. 'My daughter was watching [the film] *Chameli* on TV and suddenly she asked me, "Was my birth mum a prostitute? Was she bad and will I end up like her?"' says Varsha. Adoption expert Vinita Bhargava calls this 'passive search'—something that the child does as she grapples with differences between herself and her adoptive parents.

Now in her twenties, Varsha's daughter never felt the need to go looking for her birth parents. 'She has met people who have come and said, "There's a hole in my heart which will never heal till I meet my birth mother." Her response is always that the grass seems greener on the other side. It's been nothing but passive interest on her front,' says Varsha.

That does not mean her daughter didn't have her Que Sera Sera questions. There were lots of questions about whether she would grow as tall as the biological older brother, whether she would inherit the family's tendency not to put on weight, and so on. But there were also more searching questions about identity and abandonment. 'She would frequently ask me, "Why was I given up?" It came up before teenage,' remembers Varsha. Between eight and twelve years, she also became conscious of the various differences between her and her adoptive family. Like Trisha, Varsha's daughter too isn't as academically brilliant as her academic parents. And like Sohom and Debjani's daughter Troyee*, she too is an excellent singer. 'She would say things like, "I am not as bright as you but I can sing much better. Maybe I would have been closer to my birth family,"' remembers Varsha. 'These feelings were very common between the ages of eight and twelve.'

Sohom and Debjani also faced the birth parent search when their daughter Troyee entered her 'aggressive phase in the early teens'. It was a tumultuous time both for parents and child and it prepared the ground for more aggressive behaviour over the next ten years. 'She wanted to see her biological mother,' remembers Debjani. 'There was great fear in me—I did not know what to anticipate. Then we said, "You have to ask the lady running the agency if you want those answers," and Troyee said, "No."'

Troyee's turbulent teens also saw her going through a phase when she 'hated her biological mother'. Though her parents explained that the biological mother must have had to go through a great deal of trauma to give up her child, Troyee would oscillate between clingy insecurity ('Promise me you'll never leave me') and sheer anger ('When I have a child, I will never do to her what my biological mother did to me'). Her parents handled the situation by being determinedly consistent—they stuck to the version that the birth mother must have been under duress to give up the child and that the adoptive parents alone couldn't resolve the issue; it had to be resolved through contact with the agency. They also prepared themselves for her often extremely aggressive behaviour by finally taking the 'nature part of the story on board'.

Jayanti says the nature and nurture debate is an old one and perhaps will never end but she believes nurture is more important than nature. In many ways I buy that optimism—as an adoptive parent I would like to believe that how I bring up my child and the values with which I help her grow up will form a pull stronger than whatever her genes may have in store for her. Funnily enough, adopted kids often display characteristics that run in the family. My daughter Kiki, for instance, has inherited my mother's love of music and my husband's sense of rhythm. And Jayanti says Torsha did many of the things that she herself or her mother did as a child—the similarity was so obvious, it almost seemed like a pattern. Is this coincidence or does the nature versus nurture debate have more to it than experts have discovered so far? But that optimism aside, it's a truth that parents of children facing emotional tumult need to get the 'nature' angle on board. (This subject is discussed in greater detail in Chapter 5: Teen Tantrums).

Some parents also believe it's not necessary to reveal some particularly hateful aspects of their past to their children. Sudha and Purab, for instance, are very clear they will not reveal how she was found by the agency to their daughter Sunaina*. 'We will not tell her about being discovered abandoned at the railway station,' says Sudha. 'The saddest thing in adoption is the feeling of rejection. So we tell her that somebody left her in the agency because they loved her and wanted her to have a better life and wanted us, parents and child, to come together and stay together,' she adds.

Though western experts say withholding information is not a good idea, their reasons may not be valid in India. As discussed, Indian adoption agencies sometimes have very little information to offer either the child or the adoptive parents about the birth parents and the circumstances of the child being put up for adoption. Unlike western adoptive parents who are in constant touch with the birth mother even before the baby is born and often stay in touch with her throughout their life, there's no contact between the birth mother and adoptive parents in India. So not divulging a particularly painful nugget may not be a bad idea. As long as the child knows she's adopted and knows the agency from where she's been adopted, there's no harm in not disclosing whether the agency rescued her from a railway station or some other public place. The parents can say, 'We don't know any more and if you want answers you will have to go to the agency. If you want to go, we will come along with you and help you in your search.'

The search for the birth parents is something that is 'resolved throughout the lives of the child and the parents', says Debjani. It's not a one-time solution. But parents also need to resolve their own insecurities when the birth parent quest crops up. Adoptive parents are typically conscious parents. They want to do things right. They want to, as far as possible, mitigate any negative influence that may lurk in the child's past. So the quest for the birth parent can be as traumatic for the parents as it is for the child. Debjani remembers how for a long time she used to fear that the biological mother would come back and claim her child. That fear—most acute in the months between the time when she first saw her baby till the court order of legal guardians came their way—returned when Troyee started asking questions about her birth mother. Troyee is a naturally talented singer and is not academically brilliant, unlike the rest of her family. So, like Varsha's daughter, she would often wonder if she was 'meant to be in this family after all'. And each time she raised the issue, her mother went to pieces.

Adoption experts say the birth parent angle could also be an intrinsic part of the trauma and grief in older abused children. In her seminal book *Attaching in Adoption,*

Deborah Gray writes that there can be a bond between such children and their birth parents even if the birth parents were responsible for neglecting or abusing them. 'Adopted children may also feel a bond with their birth parents, although they may never have formed an attachment with them,' she writes. 'Their shared biologic and emotional connection with birth parents creates a bond.'

II

The other aspect of 'talking adoption' is of course to whom, in the wider society, the adoption story is be to disclosed, as well as how much of it. Most adoptive parents are proud of the fact that their child is adopted and tend to make it an open secret. Friends and family as well as the school know that the couple has an adopted child. But no one is likely to introduce their child to a rank stranger saying, 'This is my daughter and she is adopted.' (The extent and nature of disclosure to the world outside is discussed in greater detail in Chapter 7: Networking).

Informing the School

The kind of school you choose for your child will have a significant role to play in your decision to involve them in participating in some of the child's crucial emotional crises. Some new age schools like New Delhi and Gurgaon's well-known The Shri Ram School have enough adopted kids on the rolls to make an effort to sensitize the environment to their needs. Parents and the school administration keep the teachers in the loop and they make an effort to not treat adopted kids any differently, thus weeding out both negative and affirmative biases. What the teachers are trained to do is pick up telltale signs of any kind of disorder—learning disability, autism, Asperger's syndrome—and immediately alert the counsellor for expert advice. The counsellor watches the child in class for several days and, once convinced, alerts the parents and advises the necessary medical tests.

Facilities like these help kids with any special needs but since some adopted kids may also have special needs, the two are sometimes not mutually exclusive. The school's special education needs department offers the children personal attention in the form of a teacher who is attached to them and helps them solve problems they find difficult to tackle. Rather than excluding special needs kids from the mainstream, schools like these use the inclusive education method where the child gets more personalized attention to help him get over his difficulties. These kids are also offered special classes and finally, if the learning disability is severe, advised to opt for special levels where he has to drop subjects rather than go for the usual ICSE or CBSE courses available for general students.

What also helps is that adopted kids get special points during admission so getting into a school of your choice could actually be just a wee bit easier for your adopted child. Along with a sibling studying in the school, alumni kids, neighbourhood kids, adopted kids also get points during admission—all of which add up during the final calculation.

Torsha's father Pronnoy says he feels lucky that his daughter's school takes a proactive interest in handling situations specific to adopted kids. The school has an alternate or adoptive parents group and several counsellors from among its faculty and the group meet from time to time to discuss issues like disclosure, the nature/nurture question, questions about the reproductive system and being born from the tummy, questions about birth parents and handling abuse or bias from peer groups or the larger world. 'The meetings are really great because just the sharing of experiences is very reinforcing and empowers you to cope with many of these issues,' says Pronnoy. In effect it offers the parents a separate and more specific platform through which they can network with other adoptive parents in the school, share notes, and exchange ideas with them. It's particularly helpful since the school environment is so crucial for the child. His closest friends are from school, he spends most of his time in school, and these relationships will endure for the next decade and a half.

So if your child is lucky enough to get into one of these schools—though there's no affirmative bias, many of these schools do not have any negative bias against adopted kids either—then your job becomes a lot easier. The parents can then actively cooperate with the school in hand-holding the child through peer bias, difficulty with schoolwork, identity issues, and the emotional tumult of teenage compounded by the child's curiosity about her birth parents. Jayanti and Pronnoy, for instance, actively participate in the parent support activities at Torsha's school to help the teachers and counsellors understand their child's special needs. A teacher in another new age school herself, Jayanti understands both sides of the story and can bring her experience as an adoptive parent to bear upon her own school's handling of adopted children.

The trouble is, if you are in one of the metros, chances of getting into one of these institutions—arguably the best in the city—will be akin to winning a lottery. Madhumita and Probir, for instance, had a harrowing time hopping from one interview to another for Preeti's school admission. Parents are known to be reduced to nervous wrecks and one particularly antsy parent I know actually called every conceivable friend and acquaintance to get information about the school of his choice for his son. Thankfully the child cleared the test so the father did not need to move on to Plan B, C, or D.

So what do you do if your child does not manage to get into a new age school? You could do what Radhika Bawa did nearly two decades ago. Back then, adoption wasn't quite as common as it is now so the school environment was not nearly as sensitized as it is today. Radhika conducted workshops and programmes for her daughter's teachers not only to tell them about the special needs of an adopted child but also to understand their biases and points of view. That's how she came to know about the shocking prejudices some of the teachers had about adopted children—that they are all slow learners, that they are disruptive, that they are generally 'difficult' children.

You could also check with the school whether they are at least 'willing' to be sensitized to the special needs of an adopted child even if the school environment currently does not have a provision for adopted kids. Some schools may not have the provision because there are not that many adopted kids on the rolls. Others may not want to make any extra effort and can categorically tell you that when you enquire. A close friend of mine had a problem like this because her daughter is borderline autistic. The child was admitted in one of the more well-known convent schools in Delhi but when the authorities realized her special needs, they requested the mother to move the child. 'They told me they understand that my child needs special help but they are not equipped to give it and nor are they willing to invest in it because there aren't any other autistic children in the school,' my friend told me. She then moved her child to a new age school in Noida and has been much happier since. 'At least the teachers are willing to listen to the concepts that my daughter's doctor and I share with them,' she says. 'That's a beginning.'

At any rate it's a good idea to keep the school informed so that they understand some of the special needs of the child, particularly at crucial points when she may be emotionally vulnerable. For instance, if her grades suffer at the time that she's going through disclosure, the teachers should understand that she's handling something that's emotionally extremely upsetting for her and that her grades will bounce back once she's sorted things out and come to terms with the issue.

Of course not all parents believe that the school should be kept in the loop. Probir and Madhumita, for instance, feel that disclosure should be on a need-to-know basis. According to them, feedback from baby Preeti's crèche or playschool has consistently proved that she's a social, independent child and there is no need to 'colour' the school's vision with the knowledge that she's adopted. At this point, the parents feel, the school simply does not need to know.

For our part, we have always kept the school informed, if not the specific class teachers. It's a little bit like keeping the paediatrician informed—the school administration needs to know as much as they can about the child so that they can handle any instance of abuse or bias. Telling the teachers is then up to the school authorities.

Should the Wider World Know?

Adoptive parents often wonder how far the disclosure should extend when it comes to their wider circle of friends and acquaintances. While researching for this book I met scores of parents who openly shared their parenting stories with me. Many talked about grappling with serious psychological problems, others talked about working out ways to prevent any emotional manipulation, and still others discussed medical problems, the ups and downs at school, and bias in the immediate family. Yet when I asked them about being 'quoted' in the book, most parents said they did not wish to be named for the sake of their children. Reason: though the adoption issue is well established and frequently discussed at home and in their immediate surrounding, the kids still did not want the fact to be disclosed in a public forum. As Sohom explained, 'We have to make sure we do not disturb our daughter's privacy—she may not like being turned into a case study on adoption.' The parents talked about these issues because they are important and they are comfortable in their knowledge that they have either sorted them out or are in the process of sorting them out. But the children don't deserve to be subjected to the glare of public scrutiny and hence nearly every name has been changed.

Also, nearly all the parents I spoke to were clear that they did not wish to tell me anything that they have not already discussed with their children. One parent, for example, had a long and involved discussion with her adopted daughter on whether the birth mother was from a disadvantaged background and if it would impact the future of the child. But when I asked her if the baby was in fact abandoned, she replied, 'I cannot disclose that because I haven't talked about it with my daughter.' Disclosing family secrets to perfect strangers before talking about it with the child may not be a good idea. The child may wonder why his parents think he should learn about himself from a public source. It may create trust issues between the parents and the child, with the latter wondering what else is being kept from him.

All this reveals another classic dilemma for adoptive parents—till what point is it okay to be publicly open about the issue of adoption? After all, this involves yourselves and your child and she may not like the idea of being a case study. So is it okay to talk or write about the adoption, blog about it, or even tweet about it? Will it upset the child if you do? As adoption expert Vinita Bhargava points out, 'Adoptive families in India are still grappling with these questions.'

As in everything about parenting, this issue too throws up different parenting solutions. Often the disclosure happens by default. When some of my husband's professional peers congratulated me after baby came home, their wives would often say, 'We didn't even know you were expecting a baby—you didn't look it.' I would then tell them our baby is adopted. The initial message that we sent out after baby came home also mentioned the adoption angle but since then we don't mention it unless specifically asked. Our family—both immediate and extended—know that our baby is adopted. So do our friends. Beyond that, we don't feel it's necessary to trumpet the fact. After all, when a biological baby is introduced, you hardly add the 'she's biological' tag after her name, do you?

The way we look at it is that we are very proud of our daughter and it is a beautiful fact that she's adopted. It's not something we hide from anyone but it's not something we would discuss with strangers either. It's simply not relevant. It's like discussing whether ours was a love match or an arranged one. It's not a secret but it's a private matter. Those who need to know, do. Others are told when they ask or if the situation demands it.

Like us, Jayanti too thinks of disclosure as a private matter—something that's best left with the family and close friends. Her logic is the same as mine: 'It's not a secret—it's a beautiful truth and we are very proud of it. But I don't advertise that fact that my son is biological so why should I advertise the fact that my daughter is adopted?'

Adoption experts in the West say parents have to be careful about how much they discuss in public. After all, parenting is also an intensely private experience. While it is not a great idea to parade the adopted status to the world, it is also not a great idea to stay tight-lipped about it because it may make the child wonder if it is something to be ashamed of.

Ultimately, how much and how often you disclose remains an entirely private choice. It differs from parent to parent. For instance, I have decided to include instances and inferences from our experience with Kiki in this book even though most of the other names have been changed for the sake of privacy. My logic is that my child is still too small to be affected by this intrusion into her personal privacy—I would certainly not have done it if she was already a teenager, for instance. Bhargava too toes that line. 'If the child is very young, talking about adoption doesn't matter to her,' she says. 'But in middle school years, the need to fit in is very crucial so the child may not like it very much if you shout about it from the rooftops.' During teenage and early adulthood, many kids would rather not discuss the 'adoption issue' with anyone outside the family. Adoption experts say kids go through a troubling time in their teens and early twenties so any discussion of their identity can be deeply disturbing.

Interestingly, adopted kids themselves feel very comfortable talking about adoption when they are older, in their thirties or forties, and have children of their own. Take the case of Gloria*, wife of my husband's British friend Chris*. An adopted child herself, Gloria now has a biological daughter and is completely comfortable talking about the 'subject of adoption'. Her daughter Alice* is six months older than Kiki and we would sometimes exchange notes on parenting when we met socially. On one such occasion, I was anguishing about whether it was 'normal' for me to feel angry at times for being completely housebound and baby focused 24x7. Gloria laughed and said, 'Look, I am adopted and my baby is biological. I can tell you these differences are strictly in people's heads. I used to get really angry with my baby for keeping me up night after night. I am a mum but I am also human.'

Gloria was also completely comfortable talking about her identity as an adopted child. Growing up with biological siblings, having a biological child made her comfortable with her identity—she had no problems disclosing the fact that she was adopted to me, a social acquaintance, but only because my baby too is adopted. She wouldn't shout it from the rooftops but she sees no reason to keep it a secret either.

Some parents say when the question of adoption is very freely discussed within the family and friends' circle, the child feels comfortable with the concept and less hyper about disclosure. Take Lancelot Cutinha and his wife Sheela. The couple, who have two biological daughters, adopted baby girl Brigitte a couple of years ago. Lancelot feels the issue of adoption is no big deal in the family because right at the outset, the couple never felt uncomfortable telling their parents, family members, or friends about adopting Brigitte. They truly believed they had taken one of the best decisions of their lives and both sets of parents and their wider circle of friends were happy to learn about it. That openness, they feel, will make Brigitte comfortable with the idea of being adopted when she is old enough to understand what it means.

The comfort level is important particularly if parents are discussing the adoption issue in front of the child. In Jayanti and Pronnoy's case, their eight-year-old daughter Torsha had heard enough about Palna babies to patiently listen to a part of my conversation with her parents on adoption before deciding that playing with Kiki was more interesting. But Sohom and Debjani had to be more careful while discussing their teenage daughter's behavioural problems. The couple said that their daughter would not like it if she found out that she was being 'discussed'. The disclosure issue can also have an impact on the adopted child's love life with the adoptee wondering at what stage she should tell her boyfriend that she is adopted. (This issue is discussed in greater detail in Chapter 5: Teen Tantrums).

As for me, I believe this book will help my daughter understand me better when she's old enough to search for answers. It will help explain my mistakes and stumbles as much as it will help me make sense of my parenting journey. Right now Kiki is too small to understand. When she grows up, she will, hopefully, be able to make sense of the hows and whys of her parents a little better thanks to this book.

5

Teen Tantrums

TEENAGERS, ONE HARRIED parent once told me, are not the nicest people to live with. They can be prickly, they sometimes have more baggage than an airport carousel, and they genuinely believe the world—read parents—are out to make their lives as difficult as humanly possible. More often than not, they hear nothing more than the sound of their own voice and they can be notoriously difficult to either temper or discipline. Yep, living with a teenager ain't easy. That rather damning account came from a biological mum. Imagine how much more complicated the picture becomes when the teenager also has his adoption identity to handle, over and above the hormone haze he's already grappling with.

Most parents of grown-up kids I spoke to admitted children start getting antsy from middle school onwards and the rebellious streak can get really challenging by the time they are in their early teens. As for adopted kids battling serious behaviour problems, their tantrums continue all through the teens and well into the early twenties. For kids with no particular behaviour problems, the rocky patch normally lasts till the mid- to late teens. By the time they are in their twenties, they sort their problems out and make peace with themselves.

There are so many horror stories about adopted kids with behaviour problems that it's almost a cliché. The truth, though, may well lie somewhere in the middle. Not all kids who throw tantrums have serious behaviour issues. Some are just plain spoilt rotten. A schoolteacher with decades of experience handling kids with special needs in one of Delhi's premier new age schools says, 'Not all spoilt kids are adopted but a lot of adopted kids tend to be spoilt.'

So how should parents treat teenage tantrums? What are the telltale signs they should look out for that can tell them their child has a serious behaviour problem and needs medical attention? How does the parent handle verbal hurt and the emotional tumult of a child going through puberty and disclosure, all at the same time? How does the parent discipline the child without letting him raise the adoption issue to avoid censure? How does the parent get around emotional manipulation?

In adopted children, the emotional turbulence during teenage can affect schoolwork and make the child emotionally and sexually very vulnerable. How the parents handle this challenge and how correctly they read the warning signals, if any, determines how quickly the child gets help when he needs it, including counselling, therapy, or even more focused medical treatment.

That said, it's not necessary that all teenage tantrums merit special professional attention. Teenage is a difficult time for the child and the double whammy of hormones and a crisis of identity makes it even more challenging. But nine out of ten times, kids go through the turbulence and emerge stronger and more able to take on the world. All they need is consistency, patience, and some good old-fashioned hand-holding.

Adoption and Delinquency

Among the nastiest instances of bias I have faced since Kiki came home came from two people at very different points of the social spectrum. One was an elderly artist and the other the CEO of a manufacturing company. Both trotted out examples of delinquent behaviour by adopted kids to reinforce the power of nature over nurture. Both instances involved patient and competent parents and a loving, nurturing family. Yet in both cases, the kids had turned out horribly wrong.

As an adoptive parent, I am naturally inclined to believe that I can right whatever wrongs my baby's genes may have in store for her. But researching for this book has also made me understand that *sometimes* only love is not enough. Delinquent behaviour in children almost always has a trigger—sometimes, particularly if the child has been adopted at toddlerhood or later, it may be because of some trauma or abuse he was exposed to. At other times it could well be something that happened before the child was born.

Deborah Gray, in her book *Attaching in Adoption*, writes that children 'without parent figures in their first year of life have been found to have high levels of cortisol which is produced in response to stress hormones and serves as a measure of stress. Their brains are on high alert. They develop hyper-vigilant capacities at the expense of other learning.' Professor Daniel Close, Program Director, Family and Human Services in Counselling Psychology at the University of Oregon, takes that theory a step further. 'If the pregnant mother experiences prenatal stress, the stress hormone cortisol kicks in a series of brake and acceleration cycles,' he says. 'Being exposed to such high levels of spurt and spike in stress hormone in the mother's womb can cause tantrums and behaviour problems later on.' He also says there's a chance that such babies may develop cardiovascular problems and hypertension as they grow up. 'You have to take into account the possibility that every adopted baby has been exposed to stress prenatally so as parents and therapists you need to give them 20 per cent more,' he says.

Prenatal exposure to the stress hormone is only part of the story. The other, more worrying, aspect is prenatal exposure to drugs and alcohol. Western clinical experts say foetal alcohol syndrome (FAS) or foetal alcohol effect (FAE) can lead to serious neurological problems at worst and behavioural problems at the very least. Parents handling severe tantrums and behaviour issues need to take this part of the story into account instead of blaming themselves for not doing things right.

Sohom and Debjani went through absolute hell when their only daughter Troyee started acting up. A beautiful girl now in her twenties, Troyee was adopted in her infancy. Through her childhood her behaviour was normal, peppered with the 'little-more-than-usual' number of tantrums kids throw to get their way. But by the time she entered her early teens, she got into a really aggressive phase. Though it did not coincide with the disclosure period, that's when she insisted on meeting her biological mother, while at the same time professing hatred for her (*see section below*). The parents reacted initially by increasing the love quotient and being patient with her almost daily outbursts. But this search for the biological mother also made Debjani extremely nervous. It was like a Damocles sword hanging over their head—what would happen if Troyee preferred her birth mother to her adoptive parents?

For all her rebellious streak, though, Troyee did not actually want to find out more about her birth parents. After years of being beaten up with the threat, when Debjani finally said, 'We don't know anything about your birth parents so if you want we can ask the agency,' Troyee said, 'No'. Professor Dan Close feels Troyee's acting out could be the result of some prenatal exposure to stress. Her face-offs with her mother in particular got uglier and uglier till she would block every instruction and suggestion from her saying, 'You are not my real mother…who are you to tell me what to do?' Debjani initially reacted by internalizing her hurt and just going silent. 'I wouldn't try to reason with her…just let the pain come out,' she says. Later, after Troyee had calmed down, she would initiate a discussion and quietly make it clear that what she had done was unacceptable.

The ding-dong battle took a toll on Debjani and she needed meditation and spiritual guidance to cope with it all. In the end, she realized that she needed to undergo a transformation for this cycle of hurt to end. 'As parents, it is our duty to resolve her separation,' she says. She also found a way to handle hurtful manipulation by Troyee by telling her, quietly and without losing her calm, 'You cannot torment us like this. If you really want to resolve the issue of your birth parents, let us go to the agency to resolve it.' Troyee's 'you're not my mum' outbursts gradually tapered off from that point on.

Troyee's aggressive phase also coincided with a growing gap between her and her father. Till she was about eight–ten years old, father and daughter shared a beautiful, if adulatory, relationship. But as Troyee entered her teens, she slowly pushed her father to the periphery of her life. Sohom was understandably upset but took it in his stride as something all dads have to endure when their baby girl grows into teenhood and womanhood. By the time Troyee got out of her teens and her high school, Sohom worked out a way of trying to let go of her. But even in pre-college and later years, Troyee needed her family around, partly because she has never been academically brilliant and has always struggled with schoolwork.

Professor Close feels that it's a credit to Troyee's parents that she hasn't done very much worse than temper tantrums and an identity crisis. Kids with her kind of problems can easily take to drug or alcohol abuse, particularly since she has not had any therapy either. Troyee's parents realized, towards the latter half of her teenage, that her tantrums were not all the usual hormone horrors. Without informing her, they started to read up on behavioural problems in adopted kids and came to the conclusion that there's a significant role that genes can play in any adoptive scenario, as can trauma experienced in the early stages of a child's life. They realized Troyee's behaviour issues were most probably related to not what happened to her after she came to her adoptive home but what her birth mother may have faced when she was pregnant with Troyee or what the child herself faced immediately afterwards. 'We realized that there could be cognitive or affective problems and even genetic depression,' says Debjani. 'The trauma that the child endures at birth will likely explain how rocky her adolescence will be. Depression among young adults is not uncommon but the question that adoptive parents must find the answer to how the story of adoption precipitates it.'

Professor Close describes the 'acting out' behaviour as a 'fight or flight' syndrome. A coercive family process in early infancy/toddlerhood or early childhood can manifest itself over a long period through whines, tantrums, and behaviour problems. Children who are victims of abuse will either fight or throw tantrums and/or resist any instructions or rules in the household. Or they will use flight by withdrawing and shutting down the window of their emotions. That way they can shut out what they don't like, and enter what Deborah Gray calls a 'nothing feeling' or a feeling of dissociation.

In Troyee's case, the reason why her acting out started late, in her early teens, could be because 'girls tend to be "internalizers" and suffer in silence while boys act out, yelling and screaming and hitting out', says Professor Close. Girls tend to bottle it in till it all bursts out when hormones kick in at teenage.

Professor Close says parents have to look out for tell-tale signs of trauma or abuse. 'If there's a problem with early bonding and attachment, kids will tend to have impulse control problems,' he says. To correct that they need the love and guidance of their parents. But they also need therapy. Usually parents are the first to notice signs that their child's behaviour needs therapy. The trouble is often they simply don't want to go down that road. Therapy and counselling isn't as common in India as in the West and there's a strange stigma attached to it. Sohom and Debjani, for instance, tried to get a handle on the situation by 'getting a meaning into Troyee's life'. They encouraged her to focus on her singing, took her to various cultural and artistic dos (both exhibitions as well as networking opportunities) and also introduced her to satsang and meditation so that Troyee would have enough in her life to keep her busy and excited about the future.

They never told their daughter that she could be suffering from depression.

Of course not all behaviour problems are necessarily genetic or triggered by trauma. There's sometimes a more prosaic reason for them as well. Debdutta Biswas*, a teacher in one of Delhi's premier schools, says that sometimes conscious parents are also indulgent parents. In trying to do everything by the book, they often overlook bad behaviour or use an adult response to it. A very small child will not understand complicated concepts like 'We love you but we are angry with your naughty act.' Sometimes all that the child needs is something very basic. 'Parents need to understand that biological or adopted, kids need to be disciplined—kindly and consistently, as opposed to harshly and inconsistently,' says Debdutta.

So it's not necessary that all adopted kids will have behaviour issues. Sometimes their tantrums are the result of overindulgence. But sometimes the acting out is a sign of more serious trauma and abuse. Parents can work with a larger support group like the school counsellors and teachers and parents of the friends in their child's play group to get a clearer picture of how she behaves when they are not around. Sharing notes and experiences is a good way to quickly get the hang of the problem, in case it is serious enough to merit therapy.

What's also important is for parents to have control over their own feelings of inadequacy and guilt, should there be any serious behaviour problems in the child. Radhika Bawa, whose now teenage daughter Trisha also had behaviour issues, looks back on her parenting style with pride. 'I never had guilt,' she says. 'If I had to do it all over again, I wouldn't have done a better job.'

The 'I Hate My Birth Parents' Phase

While explaining the adoption story, Sohom and Debjani took care to portray their daughter Troyee's birth mother as someone who, for some reason, was incapable of looking after *any* child, not just her. They explained to Troyee that they truly did not know why her birth mother gave her up but it could be because she was unwell or in a situation that did not allow her to take good care of her baby. 'We told her that she put her child's future first, above her own need to keep her baby with her,' says Debjani. 'We tried to explain to her that she was not abandoned but handed over to someone who could ensure a better life for her.'

Yet as she grew up, Troyee went through a phase of intense hatred for her birth mother. She would often tell her mum that she never wanted to have kids—after all, she never wanted them to go through the pain of being abandoned like herself and she simply didn't know if her 'genes' would force her to be a 'bad mother'. Later she came around to the idea of having kids of her own, saying, emphatically, that she would never give them up like her birth mother did.

Varsha Bhatia's teenage daughter, on the other hand, would wonder if there was something shameful about her antecedents that made her adopted parents not disclose more. She would wonder if her birth mother was a prostitute and whether her genes would compel her to take after her birth mother. These questions of identity haunted her right through middle school to her late teens. They came juxtaposed with questions on height, physical likeness, and academic inclinations.

Handling questions about the birth parents, in particular the birth mother, can be tough for the adoptive mother. Since there's no script to this story—many adoptive parents of teenagers are first-timers in their generation and so don't have either the wealth of experience of fellow parents or the power of precedent to fall back on—parents have had to depend on trial and error to find their way ahead. Radhika

Bawa, for instance, would be wracked by tremendous fear about her daughter Trisha's learning difficulties. 'I didn't know if I was handling it right…I would often wonder, "Am I overprotecting her—am I overcompensating?"' she remembers. For an extremely bright career woman it was also a question of confidence—this was simply a project that had to work.

Right through Troyee's tumultuous teenage, the parents steadfastly remained consistent. Their stories and explanations did not change. 'Troyee would often yo-yo between hating her birth mother and wanting to meet her and see if she would be happier with her,' says Debjani. 'But we would always tell her that her biological mother must have had to go through a lot of trauma and she must have had her own compulsions for giving up the child.' Typically, she says, Troyee's outbursts against her birth parents would often be followed by great insecurity. 'She would keep telling me, "Promise me you will never leave me"… She had a great insecurity about being abandoned which she carried with her right through her teens and it's possibly lurking somewhere under the surface even now,' says Debjani.

That did not stop either Troyee or Trisha from manipulating the adoption angle to win an argument or get their way. Troyee in particular went through a phase when everything came under inquisition. As discussed above, she would question her parents' authority to censure her, saying, 'Don't tell me what to do, you are not my real parents.' But when, after putting up with it for several years, the parents suggested she go to the agency and settle the issue 'once and for all', the tantrums stopped. 'The story of adoption is also about manipulation,' says Debjani. 'If you allow that once, there's no end to it. So you've got to stop it.'

In many children, though, questions about birth parents are born out of mere curiosity. Varsha Bhatia's daughter, for instance, only ever entertained a passive interest in her birth parents. She would meet other adopted kids who would say things like 'There's a hole in my heart that will never heal till I meet my birth mother' but her reaction would be that the grass is always greener on the other side. Indeed people like Nancy Mulligan*, who travelled all the way from Canada to Chennai and the tiny village on the city's outskirts to meet her birth parents, came away distinctly underwhelmed. If anything the meeting convinced her that her 'real' mother could be any of the frail Indian ladies she met but her 'own' mother is her Canadian adoptive parent. She simply had nothing in common with her blood relatives and their milieu.

But how do parents handle a teenage child who says he hates his birth parents for abandoning him? By explaining that the birth parents, particularly the biological mother, must have had compelling reasons for doing what she did. And that she was in a circumstance that made it difficult for her to raise any child and so it is not his fault that he was put up for adoption. Unlike the West, Indian agencies don't offer too much information about birth parents—a name and reason for adoption are most commonly offered if the child wishes to know more. The law also does not mandate that the child stay in touch with his birth parents and often it is impossible to do so. But parents can help bring closure to the issue by making it clear that no matter how tough and tumultuous it is, this is one issue he will need to resolve in order to move on. Parents need to be consistent. Parents need to be kind and patient but also firm. There's no other way of handling the situation.

Disciplining the Teenager

One harried parent I spoke to while researching for this book joked that disciplining a teenager is a little bit like belling the cat. It needs to be done but, by Jove, it's a tough task. Schoolteacher Debdutta Biswas's opinion on overindulgence by adoptive parents—so much so that 'basic rules of the parenting game fly out of the window'—bears reiteration here. 'Despite all the complications of disclosure and identity, parents still need to lay down the rules and stick to them,' she says. 'Excusing all acting up as the result of past trauma means that you cut out one very basic ingredient from your parenting style—discipline.'

There's a reason why adoptive parents indulge their children. First, the entire process of seeking a child and getting her through adoption involves a conscious choice and for many couples it comes after years of childlessness so the child they get at the end of the process becomes unbearably precious. Also, most adoptive parents are conscious parents so the parenting process itself is more self-conscious.

Adoptive parents themselves agonize over this wondering, constantly, whether they are 'handling things right'. Adoptive parents like Radhika Bawa and Varsha Bhatia admit that they often have to consciously remind themselves not to 'overparent' their children. Getting a lot of focused attention is a good thing but too much of a good thing can also cause problems. All through her daughter Trisha's worst behaviour phase, Radhika Bawa would wonder if she was overparenting her child. A successful career woman, she was worried she would confuse her parenting objectives with her desire to do as well as a parent as she did in the workplace. 'I would constantly wonder if I was compensating too much,' she remembers. 'Was this a prize project for me, something that just *had* to work?'

As a teacher Debdutta has seen how quickly kids with no serious behaviour issues but a basic attitude problem settle in when they are faced with an environment that is not as forgiving as their home. Debdutta says she is sometimes appalled at how some adopted kids talk to their parents in front of teachers and counsellors. 'Yet these kids have no adjustment problems in school. They are all well settled in their peer group. But they act up at home and fling the "I am adopted" stand at parents.' This phase, though, lasts through middle school—from third to sixth standard. 'By the time they reach high school, they are firmly put in their place by their peers,' she says. By then, those with serious cognitive problems tend to become loners with one or two very close friends. Take Troyee, Sohom and Debjani's daughter. After a very rocky teenage, Troyee was not very comfortable moving to a new city post-high school to do her graduation studies. She was quite insecure about leaving her parents and agreed to move only when her mother decided to accompany her.

Behaviour problems aside, how do parents discipline a teenager when he uses the 'you are not my real parents' angle to escape censure? Most adoptive parents I spoke to stressed the need to separate the two. The idea is to tell the child that it's okay to discuss all aspects of adoption, even say hurtful stuff which is bottled inside, but not to get his way around. Troyee's case has been discussed above. Her parents went through years of torment before they finally decided it had to stop. So when Troyee tried her 'you are not my real parents' tack during one face-off, her father calmly said, 'You know as well as I do that this is the only family that we've got. You're the only child we've got, we're the only parents that you've got. So cut it out… '

Sohom and Debjani stressed the point that Troyee was free to go back to the agency to 'resolve' her tumult. That firm, no-nonsense stand helped and the manipulation came down substantially. Troyee never showed any real inclination to find out more about her birth parents from the agency. And at networking get-togethers, she would often, publicly, say, 'I don't know about adopted and biological…all I know is that my mum is the best in the world.'

All kids, adopted or biological, will manipulate a situation to gain control over it. And if the child knows that using the adoption story will get her parents to back off on studies or home chores, for instance, she will use it.

Adoption experts say parents need to be kind but *firm* to handle manipulation. 'Parenting is sometimes about being cruel to be kind,' says Debjani. 'Though you are conscious that your child is adopted and may have special needs, that doesn't mean you will not discipline her. Being adopted does not mean being pampered.' Parents need to be firm and consistent about not allowing the child to manipulate the adoption angle to get their way. For instance if the night curfew is 10 pm then the child has to return by then or there will be consequences in the form of extra chores or being grounded or less TV hours. If the child tries the 'you're being mean to me because you don't really love me and I am not really your daughter' angle, the parents need to separate the two issues without losing their calm (and therefore control over the situation). Like the Bawas, the parents can say, 'We will discuss this issue at an appropriate time if you want but right now this is about you coming back home by the curfew hour and you're going to have to stick to it. It has nothing to do with you being adopted or biological.'

Debdutta says it's normal for all children to try to manipulate the situation to get control. A biological two-year-old, for instance, routinely cried himself hoarse every morning when his mother left home for work. Yet the moment she was out of earshot, he would stop and proceed to have a perfectly normal day with no temper tantrums of any kind. It baffled the nanny no end. The child stopped his crying routine only when he started going to playschool. He enjoyed it so much that he didn't mind his mum going to work.

Some adoptive parents use a 'solution hour' to separate adoption-related anxiety from normal temper tantrums. The family sets aside an hour or so every day when parents and child sit together to discuss any adoption-related feelings that they may have. The child is allowed to voice fears, apprehensions (Was my birth mother a prostitute and will I be like her?), anger, hurt—anything that is bottled up inside. The parents hand-hold the child and help with information where possible. If the child wants, the parents can go back to the agency with her and open the file to find out more. But beyond the solution hour, the child is not allowed to use the 'I am adopted' bogey to avoid censure. If she does something wrong, she will have to suffer the consequences.

Take Varsha Bhatia's daughter who was more self-willed than her quieter biological brother. As a result she would routinely break more rules than him and get more scoldings than him. Though she did try to use the 'I am adopted so I get scolded more than Bhaiya' angle, her parents would make it clear to her that breaking the rules meant there would be consequences, adopted or not. Adoption expert Vinita Bhargava says, 'There has to be clarity about the rules in the house and that if you don't stick to them, you will be scolded. Do it more and you will be scolded more—it has to be consistent.'

One of the funniest examples of manipulation happened decades ago when a couple working overseas adopted a little girl after having a biological son. Those days adoptions were a rarity and the couple did not disclose anything to either children for a long time. The daughter, though, was finally told when she was well past her teens. The couple decided that since the sister knew, the brother also needed to know. When they told him, he wasn't surprised. 'Oh that,' he said nonchalantly, 'I knew about that. So did sis. She's been cadging things off me for years using the "if I was your real sister, you would never say no to anything I asked for" angle. I would spend half my pocket money placating her.' Clearly emotional blackmail has its fringe benefits in childhood.

Sexual Insecurities

When Trisha Bawa, Radhika and Sumit's daughter, was in her mid-teens, she had her first adolescence relationship. The boy was a neighbourhood friend and Trisha was obsessively interested in him. The relationship brought another aspect of their parenting responsibilities upfront, making Radhika and Sumit aware that their daughter needed support on multiple fronts. 'We have had to be very watchful as parents,' says Radhika. 'Trisha has always had an obsessive love interest.' Her solution was to spend a *lot* of time with her daughter, offering her emotional support. Trisha's temper tantrums—seen since childhood—got worse as her insecurity about her boyfriend increased. 'She would always agonize over how much to tell the boyfriend,' remembers Radhika. 'Should she tell him immediately after they started going around, should she wait till they got to know each other better...'

Trisha's current boyfriend is someone with whom she's comfortable in her own skin. And yes, after agonizing over the decision for months, she finally told him she's adopted and he said, 'Cool, it's no big deal.' The disclosure was like a burden off her back—Trisha felt she could now get on with the relationship without worrying about the adoption angle. Being in a stable emotional relationship has been calming for Trisha—enough to even change her ideas on having babies herself some day, something she was opposed to in her turbulent teenage. Now, she's calm enough to say she wants a baby of her own but will never give the child up like her birth mother did—no matter what.

Adoptees can look at the adoption angle as something they need to hide in order to get acceptance among their peer group. Their insecurities may convince them that the opposite sex will reject them if they find out that they are adopted. Children with behaviour issues are also typically obsessive in love. 'In all her relationships, a child like Trisha will worry about being abandoned—it will likely be a lifelong insecurity for her,' says Professor Close. Indeed, he says, the obsessive and insecure combo can be pretty troublesome for relationships with the opposite sex. 'It can scare away a lot of people.'

Varsha Bhatia's daughter, on the other hand, learnt that relationships will flounder or flourish and that adults need to take them in their stride. Her first boyfriend broke up with her after he found out she was adopted. 'He told her, "Why didn't you tell me yourself?" says Varsha. 'She said, "I didn't think it was important or relevant—I didn't tell you I have black eyes, did I?"' The first break-up was fairly traumatic for her and it also made her insecure about disclosure. Henceforth, she would always tell her boyfriends from the outset that she's adopted. But years later, she managed to settle the issue of that first break-up. 'She has finally managed to work it out in her head that the first break-up was not due to adoption alone but due to other issues as well,' says Varsha. She knows now that there are many aspects to a relationship and its fate depends on all of them—disclosure or otherwise.

Apart from the disclosure angle, adopted children can also have problems with their sexual role models. In her book *Raising Adopted Children,* adoption expert Lois Ruskai Melina says that adopted kids may have problems sticking to the parental role model, particularly if they are physically very different from their adopted parents. For instance, if the son is taller or bigger built than his father, he may have trouble looking up to his dad as a sexual role model. Similarly, if the son is sportier than the father, he may have trouble looking up to his dad as a role model. With girls, that same image issue may crop up if the adoptive parents are infertile. The pregnant daughter of an infertile mother may have trouble seeking the kind of practical help and assurance that daughters usually look for at that point in time. She may wonder whether her mum will be able to tell her how painful the labour contractions will be for instance, since she has never, herself, given birth.

While western adoption experts say the way to deal with this situation is to encourage kids to have multiple role models outside of their immediate family, this problem is less manifest in India where multicultural rainbow families are not that common. Also, given that biological children can also have role models beyond their parents—due to the closeness of the extended family and friends' circle in India—this isn't that big a deal in our context.

As for sexually abused children, again that's a context not terribly relevant in India yet since it usually crops up only with older adopted children. Adoption experts say the classic sign of sexual abuse is when a child displays sexual behaviour or knowledge completely inappropriate for his age. Children, abused or otherwise, don't really understand that they are behaving sexually—for them it is simply a means to control and manipulate the situation. 'Children control when they feel unsafe,' writes Deborah Gray in her book *Attaching in Adoption*. Also, children who have suffered trauma and abuse 'equate power with dominance and brutality…they do small things during the day to exert power over others. Often they hurt others in order to dominate.'

Like all parents, adoptive parents too need to offer simple advice on sexual education and health when their children reach puberty. Working with the school, teachers, and counsellors is a good way to make sure the discussion is open and simple enough for the child to understand and remember.

The Clingy Child, the Reserved Adolescent

For new parents, the clingy child searching for her mother or father's familiar face for comfort is a validation of sorts. It tells the parents that the child has settled in and she's started forming attachments in her new home. Attachment can be a huge issue, particularly for slightly older adoptees or children with an abused or traumatic past or medical and psychological problems. For therapists, helping the child form new attachments is a structured and well-tested step-by-step process through which the child learns to be a child once more, discarding the adult role she may have been forced to adopt.

No matter how clingy in infancy, children quickly outgrow their fear of the social unknown and make friends independent of parent supervision or presence. Induction into a playschool, for instance, will see children in varying degrees of comfort—some will settle in immediately and be happy to go to school every day, secure that their daily routine of school, home, parent time, play, feed time, sleep time will not be disrupted. Others take longer to be on their own and typically a parent needs to sit in at class or play to help the child relax.

But some children remain insecure and clingy right through their toddlerhood and into their adolescence and late teens. Their emotional confusion about their identity plus some behavioural or medical conditions may be responsible for this. Koel*, now in her twenties, had an extremely rocky teenage as she clashed with her parents Raja* and Sebanti* on pretty much everything, from choice of friends, focus on study to curfew hour. Yet, despite the almost daily spats, Koel was extremely insecure about social interaction without her parents. If she was going to a social get-together or party and did not know anybody there, she would either make excuses or want her parents to come along. And after high school when she secured a two-year course at a French university to read music, she wanted one of her parents to go along with her. In the end, her mother took a sabbatical from her high-profile job to accompany Koel to her grad school.

Some adoptive parents say they feel a conflict of emotions when they come across clinginess of this kind. On the one hand, it makes them feel good that they are still the obvious people that the child turns to for comfort and security. But on the other, they wonder how soon she will be independent and secure enough to seek adult relationships on her own, without the crutch of her parents. Western adoption experts say it's not uncommon for children with serious behaviour problems to become extremely clingy and parents need to take baby steps introducing them to independence in the form of day care or playschool. The memory of being abandoned haunts these children and makes them wonder if their parents will come back after dropping them off at day care, for instance. Their insecurity stems from their fear that they will somehow lose their parents and home once again, just as they have had to leave their birth parents or caregivers at the agency.

Experts like Professor Close suggest that in some of these cases, therapy may be a good idea to help the child resolve her feelings of being abandoned. While each kid is inherently different and special in her own way, a generally 'sensitive' and 'introvert' child could also be suffering from bipolar disorder. The problem is not specific to adopted kids—biological kids with behaviour issues or bipolar disorder will be just as withdrawn. Take the case of nine-year-old Blanchefleur*, daughter of a French father and an American mother now based in Chicago. Always known as a sensitive if quiet and introverted kid, Blanche was recently diagnosed with bipolar deficiency. Her parents had no clue till the therapist suggested specific tests. Blanche had always been a quiet if a little clingy child and her parents had always enjoyed the fact that she liked their company as much as going for pyjama parties to her friend's house. The symptoms may not be very obvious but the behaviour pattern will show up often enough for the school, counsellor, paediatrician, or therapist to suggest a test.

Sometimes, though, clinginess is yet another means of manipulation. Mandira's four-year-old son Atri turned hyper clingy when she rejoined work after a gap of about four years. She had taken a sabbatical after Atri came home and decided that she needed to wait till he started school before taking on work once more. A talented graphic designer, she was confident that she would not have problems finding work despite the four-year gap. Atri had settled in beautifully at his new kindergarten so Mandira felt confident he wouldn't mind his mother going out for work too. But Atri's reaction was unexpected. He became incredibly clingy, was depressed for months, fell ill several times including coming down with raging fever the day she started work, would imagine her boss as a Manga monster, and complained to his grandparents (Mandira's parents) that they should scold Mummy for going to work. He even started crying before going to school every morning, inventing stories of how his teachers made him stand in a corner every day.

Mandira was puzzled by this reaction. She checked with the teachers and his classmates to find that he was fibbing about school. And she felt guilty about going to work every day. Her method of driving home the message was to continue working right through Atri's frequent bouts of fever and tummy upsets. In a couple of months he realized Mummy would go to work even if he stayed at home and staying at home by himself with his nanny was not much fun. Atri took a while to get his head around this, but he finally decided going back to his old routine was a better idea. His clinginess too has come down a few notches though it hasn't gone away entirely.

Experts also say sometimes even a naturally outgoing child can become tongue-tied and clingy in a brand-new environment. In Atri's case, for instance, his mother's work routine was something he was not used to. Hence the clinginess. In many playschools, children feel insecure without at least one parent being present in their general vicinity till the school environment becomes familiar. Slightly older children may feel a bit intimidated at large social gatherings like weddings where they are exposed to a whole gaggle of relatives they may have met only occasionally. Children like routine and any deviation from routine can take a little getting used to. That holds true for all children, adopted as well as biological.

6

Fighting Prejudice

THE BIGGEST DIFFERENCE between adoptive and biological parenting is the prejudice that adoptive parents face all through their lives. The remarks can come from any quarter. Some are unintended, some deliberately hurtful. They can come from friends, family, rank outsiders, and even domestic help. The commonest ones are actually meant to be complimentary, lauding the parents for doing something 'noble'. Others can range from mildly irritating—'the baby is so lucky to have found a place in your home'—to downright offensive—'how much did you have to pay to get the child' or even 'if you waited a little longer, you could have had your own child'. The worst are those that use perfectly true incidents or case studies to bolster a bias against adopted kids. For instance, I faced a long and patronizing lecture from an acquaintance on how adopted kids can turn out to be delinquents. 'After all, genes are genes,' ended the gentleman with a flourish.

Most of these comments are born out of ignorance rather than any real ill will. Indeed as an adoptive parent I faced far less curiosity or unthinking comments than did the first generation of adoptive parents in urban India. Things were far more difficult a couple of decades ago when the only kind of adoption society knew and accepted were within-the-family affairs. The classic instance of Kunti in the epic Mahabharata—her biological father Surasena gave her away to his childless friend Kuntibhoj who became her adoptive father—is a pointer to the way popular mindset saw the issue. In the epic, Kunti grew up to bear the scars of that separation right through her unfortunate life. And tradition-bound India more or less bought that story—people simply believed that adoptees could find happiness only when reunited with their birth parents. Society felt adoptees necessarily carried the weight of being 'given up' all their lives—an emotional cross that left an imprint on their future. Popular Hindi cinema did nothing to improve this image—from the 1960s' classic *Waqt* to the 1970s' hits *Amar Akbar Anthony* or *Yaadon Ki Baraat*, the adoptive parent appeared on screen only to be thoughtlessly forgotten when the grown-up child rediscovered his 'real' parents after many intricate twists and turns in the lost-and-found tale.

Things have changed for the better since then but the bias remains, to a greater or lesser degree. How well the parents handle this and protect their children from it is one of the biggest tests of adoptive parenting. Remember, even if you bite someone's head off for saying something hurtful, it won't make your child feel any better. And there's no saying where these statements will crop up. In a sense adoptive parents must forever be on their guard to insulate their children from insensitive remarks.

Family Hostility

Nothing is more important to the adopted child than complete and whole-hearted acceptance by her immediate family and friends. In the formative years, knowing that her grandparents, uncles, aunts, and cousins love her unconditionally is a huge confidence booster and character builder for the adopted child. It gives her an armour with no chinks in it, with which to face any bias in the world outside. In the absence of that affection, things can go very badly wrong.

Take the case of Sumit and Radhika Bawa. The couple adopted a baby girl nearly fifteen years ago, when adoption was not as common even in urban India as it is now. So when their daughter Trisha came home, the couple faced resistance from one set of parents. 'We were the first generation of adoptive parents and it was hard for a middle-class family to get their heads around the concept of an alternative family,' remembers Radhika. Her parents supported their decision, his did not. Essentially it was pride in their genes—given that he comes from an academically illustrious family—that triggered the resistance. Things were even more hurtful because Radhika and Sumit were living with his parents at that time. 'It saddened us immensely,' remembers Radhika. 'We were all living together and there were these awkward silences.'

Over the years, the grandparents' resistance hit young Trisha really hard, more so because she could never match up to their ideal of an academically brilliant grandchild. The grandparents took a long, long time to come around and it was only when Trisha graduated and received an expensive heirloom as a gift that she felt she'd finally been 'accepted'. This gap in her life affected Trisha deeply and was, to some extent, responsible for much of her teenage and tweenage angst. In hindsight, Radhika says adoptive parents need to be 'totally convinced and really strong' about their decision, should they face what she and her husband faced with their child. Outside bias is easy to arm-flex away—bias in the family hurts deeply.

Radhika and Sumit's experience may be decades old but it's by no means unusual even today. Probir and Madhumita faced a similar reaction from his mother when their baby Preeti came home. Elderly and ailing, it took her a while to get used to Preeti. In fact, the two started bonding only when Probir's mother came to live with her son and his family nearly three years later.

Living with a disapproving parent or parent-in-law can be an absolute nightmare for adoptive parents. But it's deeply damaging for the child. These days the home study puts special emphasis on how the wider family will accept the child. In fact, Reema* and Abhinav*, who desperately wanted to adopt a baby girl so their biological daughter Rinky* would have a sibling, never passed muster because the home study would invariably pick up telltale nuances from the grandparents who live with the couple.

Of course sometimes the entire family roots for the baby and makes the whole experience a real celebration. When Shonali and Arun drove to the agency to bring their baby home, they were accompanied by his parents. After baby came home, Shonali's parents came over. And soon after came his brother and her sister-in law. Similarly little Lily was pretty much looked after by her maternal grandparents when Pritha fell ill immediately after baby came home. Later, when Lily met her father's folks in the UK, she took to them quickly, as they to her.

In our case, we were really lucky because both sets of parents were completely supportive from day one. Both my mother and mother-in-law are extremely fond of Kiki and she knows that she has her uncle, aunt, and cousins all wrapped around her little finger. As she grows up, I am sure she will cherish these relationships and realize how lucky she is to be surrounded by so much love.

During my chats with social workers, I have often asked them what they would advise couples who are still trying to get their parents on board. They invariably say, 'Wait till they come around. Grandparents want a grandchild almost as desperately as parents want a baby—so at some point, when they realize how much adoption means to you, they will come around.' In Arun and Shonali's case, her parents came around when they saw the toll her miscarriages were taking on her health.

Sometimes that moment when everything falls into place happens when the grandparents first see the baby. And even when it isn't love at first sight, the bonding can grow slowly, over the years. In Arun and Shonali's case, her father was won over after his first glimpse of the baby. Though he was apprehensive in the beginning, he is now so sold on his only grandchild that he literally hogs all the baby time he can when she comes visiting. Citing her own experience, adoption expert Vinita Bhargava says that the best way to get parents on board is to talk to them. 'We spoke to every single family member to get them on board,' she remembers. 'It was crucial that they understood.'

Of course having the support of close friends can often make up for parental disapproval. Even when parents aren't resistant but are separated from their grandchild by geography and circumstance (including ill health), friends can help make up for that gap. For Madhumita the initial lack of support from her mother-in-law did not matter. First, because with her and Probir sharing everything, she never felt the pressure. Also her mother, who already had both adopted and biological grandchildren before Preeti came along, was completely supportive from day one. What Madhumita treasures, though, is how their friends chipped in to make the moment of baby coming home special. Indeed acceptance of friends is something that she still treasures, even more than that of family. To Probir and Madhumita, that spontaneous show of solidarity and affection meant the world. That love and affection helped compensate for what Preeti missed out on from her grandmother. It helped make her an extremely confident child.

Even though we never had a problem of family hostility, I have seen what it is like to have whole-hearted support from friends. When Kiki came home, my closest friend Reshmi searched for patchwork quilt patterns on the net, downloaded a particularly stunning pattern, shopped for pink checks and stripes of various kinds, and handcrafted a beautiful quilt for my baby. That and the elaborate handknitted patchwork quilt from my mother-in-law and sister-in-law and a handknitted beret from my mother are all precious gifts which Kiki will doubtless cherish even when she's too old to use them.

Bias in the School

Adopted children face their biggest challenge when they leave the sheltered environment of home to start school. School is a challenge for all children—biological and adoptive—but the latter have some special issues which can make school life trying unless the teachers and the school environment are liberal and free enough to allow the child to flower. Many of the adoptive parents I spoke to, particularly those with teenage or older schoolgoing children, complained that their kids faced bias and hostility in school. Though there are schools which are particularly attuned to the needs of adopted or special needs children, most schools don't make any effort to understand the special circumstances of adopted kids.

Take Radhika and Sumit's now teenage daughter Trisha. She was never academically brilliant and though her school, one of Mumbai's top new age educational institutions, was open enough to allow her interest in art and music to flower, she still struggled with coursework. Things got so rocky that Radhika actually took some time off from her work to help her daughter cope. With hindsight, she says, left to her devices, Trisha would not even have finished school. It was her mother's constant hand-holding right through middle and high school that helped build confidence.

Having gone through all the attendant problems that come with parenting a slow learner, Radhika now says the issue of school is critical in adoptive parenting. Choosing the right school where the teachers have the right attitude is important for biological children but critical for adoptive ones. Back when Trisha was growing up, adoption was a rare enough trend and most schools simply did not know how to handle kids with learning problems. 'It was common to come across teachers who had little sensitivity and who refused to budge from their own fixed notions,' Radhika remembers.

But the biggest problem that Trisha encountered were masked biases. 'That was very difficult because it made the ground slippery—the child simply did not know what to take at face value and what not,' says Radhika. Example: the teacher may profess that she does not differentiate between biological and adopted kids, but the way she handles them in class may disclose her prejudices. Radhika remembers with horror how, while conducting an orientation programme for teachers on the issue of adoption, she came across statements like 'Adopted kids are always problematic,' 'They are all dull and can't keep up with the class,' 'Adopted kids have behaviour issues,' etc.

The situation is, of course, much better now and there are schools like The Shri Ram School in Gurgaon and Delhi which lays special emphasis on handling adopted kids with sensitivity. But The Shri Ram School and other premier schools are difficult to get into so if your child has not managed to clear the admission test for one of these new age schools, what do you do?

Madhumita's niece Pompey is a case in point. Daughter of a single mother, Pompey is a cheerful, confident child but is not traditionally academically oriented. Her mother decided to put her in a reputed school in Gurgaon but was unhappy with the streamlined academic focus so she quickly changed to a smaller, new age establishment. Turns out this one too is new age mostly in name and Pompey is extremely unhappy in her new school. Madhumita and Probir, for their part, are quite clear that they don't want to hobble their child by announcing the fact that she's adopted to her school. 'Being adopted does not make Preeti any different or special—we have had consistent feedback that she's a social child so for us it's immaterial,' she says, adding that she's not inclined to 'sensitize' the school that her child is adopted. In fact, she wants her daughter and niece to move to a boarding school when they are a little bit older. Reason: it will make them smart, it will toughen them up and they will be able to handle any situation and any kind of bias even with Mum and Dad not around. 'The peer group can be cruel and discriminating but I want the girls to be able to handle it on their own,' says Madhumita. She believes the cousins will always have each other to fall back on, a replication of the camaraderie that Madhumita herself shared with her sister right through school and college life.

Madhumita's point of view is one way of handling the school angle. The other is Radhika's. When her daughter started facing academic difficulties, Radhika decided to deal with the school, finding people who could help, and even going to clinical psychologists. The school system, she says, forces the child to conform even though every child is essentially different. For a while she even tried open school but her daughter missed the school environment enough to work with her mother on getting the academic part of school life sorted out.

For our part we have kept Kiki's school authorities in the loop from day one. When she started going to playschool, I had a long session with her school principal, informing her about the fact that Kiki is an only child and an adopted one. Ditto for her current school. For us, it's important to sensitize the school about the child's needs, if any, and like the paediatrician, we felt the school needed to understand the adoption angle.

Even if the school is a liberal, new age one—The Shri Ram School, Gurgaon, for instance, gives additional weightage to adopted children (along with neighbourhood kids and siblings or alumnus kids) and has a significant body of adopted kids on its roster—it still can't filter out peer bias. Jayanti and Pronnoy's eight-year-old adopted daughter Torsha came home in tears one day. No matter how hard she tried, Jayanti couldn't get her to reveal the reason. Finally it came out at bedtime—it seems a classmate jeered at Torsha during biology class saying, 'You don't know babies come from their mother's tummy because your mother isn't really your mom—they are not your real parents, they are only bringing you up.'

Understandably, Jayanti was furious and lodged a complaint the next day. When confronted, the guilty child's parents were dumbstruck. They had no idea where their daughter picked up something so hateful from. Though the school authorities ticked off her classmate on that occasion, Torsha knows she can never be protected entirely from these nasty remarks. But there was a positive fallout. Torsha's biological brother turned out to be her biggest confidence booster—three years younger than her, he simply announced in school the next day that he would bash up anyone who dared to hurt his sister.

Bias in the Wider Circle

Though school bias can be more harmful than anything else the child may encounter in her wider social circle, even stray comments can cause a lot of harm. I still remember a comment made by Kiki's nanny when she was all of seven months old. While explaining her diet chart to the nanny, I told her to stick to both the items and the timings of the feed. Her reply was, 'Don't worry, I have handled lots of biological babies and yours is only adopted.'

My reaction to that off-the-cuff nasty comment was to immediately fire the nanny. The trouble was she genuinely couldn't understand what she'd said was wrong. Since that experience we make sure we do not discuss the adoption issue in front of domestic help. We have no means of knowing how they will react to that information and whether it will make them feel that they don't need to give our baby the attention that is given to a biological child. More importantly I don't want my child to be the subject of larder gossip of any kind.

The incident with the nanny may have surprised us but far more annoying was the comment from a cousin who came to see our baby girl and spent a quarter of an hour waxing eloquent on how noble we were and what an example we have set in society. Fortunately Kiki was too small at that time to understand what was being discussed but it left both my husband and me extremely irritated. Finally, I had to stop him mid-flow to explain that we did not adopt a child to 'set an example' or to 'be noble'. We did it to become parents. We did not do our baby a favour by adopting her. She did us a favour by becoming our child. So we were, in fact, a very selfish couple. We adopted for entirely selfish reasons. Others like Madhumita and Probir advise adoptive parents being given the 'you are so noble' treatment to just 'take it as it comes'.

The truth is you can't insulate your world completely from insensitive remarks. Every once in a while someone will say something that is mean or nasty. Adoptive parents need to tell their children to be prepared for that chin music. Growing up isn't easy. No one will grow a bed of roses for you. So be yourself, be smart, judge people, and make friends carefully. That's the advice Madhumita's father gave his five daughters. And that's the advice she would want Preeti to inherit. 'When my sister and I joined college, we were small-town girls who wore handmade clothes in a classroom full of stylish and wealthy kids,' she remembers. The sisters were sneered at and made to feel like dorks. But it made them work doubly hard and excel in the classroom and in extracurricular activities. By the time college came to an end, no one dared to call them dorks. 'That's what I want Preeti to go through and like me she'll have Pompey for company. Always,' she says.

Vinita Bhargava says many of the questions adoptive parents attract are triggered more by curiosity than any real malice. 'Back when we adopted, it was very rare and the novelty factor was much stronger,' she says. 'So our adoption became a talking point and we faced a lot of whys—why did you do it? It was more curiosity than negativism,' she says.

A decade and a half on, Shonali and Arun are still facing the brunt of some of that curiosity. And not all of it is pleasant. Shonali says she gets asked all the time if she had pregnancy problems and if the doctor told her she couldn't conceive. Her response is more emphatic than ours: 'We did this for us and our baby did us a favour by coming home. We couldn't have children for the longest time and we didn't want to wait any more. We can have a biological child any time we want but we want to become parents right now.'

The worst of the lot are the so-called well-wishers who love to relate 'horror stories' about adopted children going astray. An elderly acquaintance went into great detail while recounting a story about a couple's adopted son going completely off-kilter despite their best efforts to inculcate the right values in him. He started out being testy, rapidly degenerated into violent and abusive behaviour, took to drugs, and finally left home at twenty-one, never to return. Their daughter, a biological child, on the other hand, was the very paragon of virtue—she completed school with straight As, went to an Ivy League college, and tried her best to drill some sense into her demented brother's head with little effect.

The trouble with stories like these is that they are mostly perfectly true. The gentleman concerned was recounting this example to establish his point that genes somehow score over environment and nature cannot be bested by nurture. I could have stopped him in his tracks with a suitably cutting reply except that most of what he was saying is also true. The nature versus nurture argument is as old as the hills and most adoptive parents go through their share of anguish and angst on that score. There are instances of adopted kids showing delinquent behaviour. There are also instances of them suffering from inherited medical problems, both physical and psychological. There are instances of adopted kids' tantrums and behavioural problems that go way beyond just teenage angst. In many cases these have deep roots in the child's genetic make-up. An adopted child has to resolve the issue of being abandoned and she does that with help from her parents. It's a lifelong resolution and sometimes it can carry on right till the time the adopted child is in her middle age and has children of her own.

Coming back to comments like the ones I encountered, the best way to handle them is to hear the person out and then politely say, 'What you are saying is perfectly true but are all criminals and delinquents in this world adopted children?' There are as many biological delinquents as adopted ones and there's no way a parent can crystal-ball-gaze into the future to figure out how her child will turn out. If we could do that, we would all pick the perfect babies but the truth is no baby is perfect. The parent does her best and hopes that the child will turn out well and will lead a healthy and happy life. If it works out that way, good enough. If it doesn't, there's nothing you can do about it. The question isn't one of adoptive versus biological. When it comes to quirks of nature, no one has any clue.

7

Networking

FOR ADOPTIVE PARENTS the biggest comfort can come from knowing that there are others who have pretty much gone through what they have and that they are not the only ones facing guilt, uncertainty, ill-health, and the other challenges that parenting throws up. As adoption becomes a real trend, particularly in urban India, adoptive parents are catching up and sharing notes more often. As an adoptive parent myself, I can vouch for how helpful that give and take can be. Networking is crucial to adoptive parenting. Given how different our parenting experiences often are compared to what our mothers or mothers-in-law went through (they were biological parents in a different social and economic milieu), it's often more useful consulting a fellow adoptive parent rather than the immediate family members. As for me, I take most of my parenting cues from my mother but I also know I cannot expect her feedback or ideas on matters peculiar to adoptive parenting. For that I turn to my wider circle of friends who are adoptive parents.

Organized and Improvised Networking

Many of the first generation adoptive parents I spoke to felt that our lot have it easy, compared to a few decades ago when only adoptions within the family were seen as acceptable. The first gen adoptive parents got around the roadblock of the prevalent mindset by building their own networks and seeking support and advice from each other. Delhi-based adoptive parents Debjani and Sohom, for instance, were one of the first to sign up for a network called Alternative Parenting Network Association (APNA). Now, Debjani acknowledges that the APNA network was extremely useful because it not only provided support when they were going through some of the most trying times in their lives as parents, but also helped them 'find broader patterns'. 'It helped us make sense of what we were going through, offered a forum where we could talk about our personal experience with others who were in a similar situation, and helped us to handhold other couples who were adopting,' she adds. APNA is a very active and prominent networking forum but it's hardly the only one. There are others that are equally well known and vocal. For instance,

ATMAJA is a registered community-based organization for adoptive parents in West Bengal. It has been working on issues related to adoption for the past ten years. Then there is the Indian Federation of Adoptive Families Associations (IFAFA) which is based in Mumbai. As an adoptive parent you can ask your agency to put you in touch with one of these associations if you feel you need to network with other adoptive parents, particularly if there aren't that many instances of adoptive families in your own social circle.

Of course if there are enough adoptive parents in your wider circle or even in the school that your child attends, you may not even feel the need to seek out organizations like APNA or ATMAJA. In our case, for instance, we were fortunate to have several adoptive families among our larger circle of friends so we never felt the need to formally align ourselves with an organization. Having adoptive families right next door meant that any time we wanted to share notes or check something out—particularly the process of acquiring baby's birth certificate from the municipal corporation, for instance or getting her passport made—help was just a phone call away. Many parents whose kids are now of school going age say they depend on the school forum to exchange notes and seek help. Pronnoy and Jayanti certainly do that with Torsha and Raju's school and say they find the note-sharing 'empowering'. Organizations like APNA or ATMAJA came in handy for the first generation of adoptive parents like Debjani and Sohom. They are also important pressure forums taking the concerns of adoptive parents to the government for policy improvements. The decision to include adoptive mothers in the maternity benefits available to government servants, for instance, was thanks to some spirited suggestions by ATMAJA. And CARA routinely stays in touch with these organizations to be in the know about the kind of concerns that the community of adoptive parents may have, which in turn get translated into policy improvements. The buffer of a larger social network was crucial as much for Debjani and Sohom as for their now grown-up daughter. 'There are special issues which concern adopted children and resolving them is as much a journey for the child as it is for the parents,' says Sohom. Adoption experts, like Professor Daniel Close, say that adopted children often carry with them traumas and memories of their biological experiences even at a neonatal or foetal state which can leave an imprint on their future.

Even if you do not have any behavioural or other issues to handle, staying in close touch with other adoptive parents is a really good idea. Reason: 'Adoptive parents are a minority,' explains adoption expert and herself an adoptive parent Vinita Bhargava. 'In biological parenting there's a set script that has come down to us through generations. But in adoptive parenting we only borrow ideas from the West which often don't fit in.' Hence the dilemma of Indian adoptive parents. Am I being the right kind of parent? Is this the right way ahead? These messages keep coming all through and because there's no set script, it's something the parents need to find out on their own. Like Sohom and Debjani, Bhargava too has, over the years, relied heavily on the support that APNA offered. 'We would meet at least once or twice a month and there was a lot of hand-holding through APNA,' she remembers. 'It helped.'

When schools encourage networking and offer a platform for parents to share their experiences, it becomes an 'empowering' experience for parents. Schools offer a close-knit community that the child will share all through his schoolgoing years covering tween, teen, and young adulthood. A school forum allows the parents to share their experiences, exchange tips, talk to the school counsellor or an adoption expert, and report bias or abuse if any. It also allows the school to keep the parents in the loop in case of any learning disability or other problems. Many new age schools in fact have alternative parenting groups which include adoptive parents as well. As the number of adopted children on their roster increases, the need for a special networking opportunity like this will be greater.

As for me, I realized even when there's no dilemma, just sharing notes with another parent helps give you a different perspective. For instance, my husband and I were very clear that we would try to make Missionaries of Charity as much an intrinsic part of Kiki's life as school and the playground. So every year, we would have a special birthday party for her at the centre and she has now come to expect that she'll have two birthday parties—one for her friends in school and another for her friends 'with the sisters'. But not all parents feel staying in close touch with the agency is necessary. Madhumita, for instance, is quite clear that she will explain the adoption issue to her child when she's old enough to understand but there's no need to keep taking her back to the agency to refresh her memory. Nor does the same script work for everyone. When Eron and Pritha tried to take baby Lily back to the agency, she reacted really badly and did not want to go anywhere near the building.

Sometimes, sharing notes or picking another parent's brain can give you real light bulb ideas. Before Kiki came home, I had a long chat with Sohom on how he handles the issue of an adopted child being somehow different. He said, 'I keep telling my daughter that there are all kinds of people in this world. There are babies with blond hair, black hair, blue eyes, green eyes, brown eyes, there are pale babies and dark babies, fat babies and thin babies. Similarly there are adopted babies and biological babies.' It struck me as a really intelligent way of handling the issue—simple and to the point. That way the child does not think she's either 'special' because she's somehow 'chosen' or she's 'inadequate' because 'she was given up'. She's just another type of child in a Benetton ad world of diversity. A month later, when the social worker asked me how I would deal with the adopted versus biological issue during the home study, I quoted Sohom verbatim. The social worker loved the concept and gave us a glowing review.

Making Friends with Other Adopted Kids

When our daughter Kiki was old enough to play in the park in our condominium complex, we would encourage her to play with Probir and Madhumita's daughter Preeti. As parents we felt that being close friends with another adopted child of the same age would not only drive home the Benetton ad theory to our baby but also give us cues on how to explain tricky issues like biologic and adopted to our child. In time, Preeti and Kiki grew very close and now that we have moved to Pondicherry,

Kiki still remembers her toddlerhood playmate and frequently asks me about her.

Preeti has always been very close to her cousin Pompey who is also adopted. Like us, her parents too want the girls to be close, not merely because they are family but also because they can be there for each other in future. Madhumita in fact wants both Preeti and Pompey to go to the same boarding school so that they can handle any rough treatment together and come out on top. In a sense Madhumita wants Preeti and Pompey to enjoy the same kind of bond that she did with her own sister—a lifelong support system, a friend, sister, companion, soulmate all rolled into one.

It is important for adopted children to have others like them around. It not only gives them confidence that they are not the only ones to be adopted, but also makes them open to experiences and ways of handling them once they are older. Indeed most of the adoptive parents I spoke to while researching for this book say, emphatically, that they encourage their children to become friendly with other adopted children. When I visited Pronnoy and Jayanti's house to interview them for this book, I took my baby along with me. Jayanti introduced Kiki to her adopted daughter Torsha saying, 'See, here's Kiki—she too is a Palna baby.' Torsha was adopted from Palna and her parents have turned the agency into a generic term for all adopted kids. I must admit I was very happy to see Kiki playing with both Torsha and her biological brother. When we left, both kids gravely instructed me to please bring baby over more often so they could all play together.

Sometimes parents need the example of other adopted kids to simply explain things to their children. Take baby Lily, who continues to be in denial though her parents have been trying to explain the concept of adoption to her. Eron and Pritha believe having more adopted children in her wider circle of friends will help Lily understand what her parents are trying to explain. 'We want Lily's play group or friends' circle to be more varied,' says Pritha. 'It'll be particularly helpful if she gets to know some older adopted children.' That way Lily will know there are other adopted kids like herself and in time she can even look up to some of the older kids as role models.

Like Eron and Pritha, single mum Rupali Mitra too is trying to make her daughter Ariana's social circle less homogeneous. Like Lily, Ariana too is grappling with the concept of adoption. She is also in denial about being a single-parent child. Rupali feels having another single-parent child in her playgroup has helped because now there's a reference point for Ariana to hang on to. She is also trying to include other adopted and single-parent kids in her daughter's larger play circle so that there are enough kids from different backgrounds for Ariana to not feel like the odd one out.

In Torsha's case, friends of her parents pitched in to make her play and social circle more varied. Jayanti remembers how adoptive parents of teenagers would offer to let their children talk to Torsha to help her grapple with some of the problems of bias she was facing in school. 'They would say, "Bring her over and let her talk to our children and see how they handle it,"' recalls Jayanti. In middle school, Torsha still does not have the confidence of a teenager but feels comforted when there are older kids who say they went through the same stuff when they were her age. What has also helped is the special needs department in her school—The Shri Ram School, Gurgaon. 'There are so many, so many adopted kids around, it's a common fact of life for Torsha,' says Jayanti.

Vinita Bhargava says that the support of a networked group can be invaluable for the children, in addition to the parents. For her, APNA meetings 'allowed the children also to meet and know that there are other adopted children. They could call up and talk to somebody and share their experiences—it's important.'

Networking is also important for inter-racial adoptions. Adoption experts feel introducing the child to people of her own racial or ethnic stock is a good way of sensitizing her to her racial identity. In fact it also gives the child enough confidence about her adopted identity to be able to search for her birth parents later in life. Nancy Mulligan is of Indian descent but her adoptive family is Canadian. Nancy has both a biological sibling as well as an adopted one. While growing up in her rainbow family Nancy was exposed to enough people of Indian origin around her to give her confidence in her own multicultural identity. When she grew up, she decided to use her gap year to travel to India in search of her birth parents. As it turns out, she didn't quite manage to meet them but did visit the village where they lived. She came away satisfied that she had less in common with the denizens of the Tamil Nadu village from where her birth parents came than her multi-cultural friends' circle back home in Montreal. When I chatted with her before she returned home to her Canadian parents, she was quite clear in her head about her identity. Yes, she is Indian in origin but she's really Canadian in every other way. Being exposed to other Indian children in her school and social circle in Canada convinced her that a dual identity isn't unusual. Nor is it a contradiction in terms.

Of course it is not unusual to come across adopted children in their teens completely rejecting the idea of mixing with other adopted children or being involved in adoption-related support groups. That's because as they grow up, children like to look out for and find friends on their own—having your parents offer you a ready social circle isn't 'cool'. The child may think he is being compelled to socialize with the group because the parents think he should. Often the only similarity he shares with other kids in the group is the fact that they are adopted whereas adolescent children look out for other commonalities such as similar interests in music or films or science or a larger common group of friends. Schoolteacher Debdutta Biswas says that though there are a fair number of adopted kids in her school, they rarely hang out with each other even if they are in the same class or playgroup. Indeed even kids that have grown up socializing with each other may end up forging their own friends' circle, distinct from their adoptive identity. If and when that happens, it's best to respect the child's choices—force-feeding friendship is never a good idea.

However, for younger kids, that exposure is important. Younger children can quickly socialize with and make friends with other kids as long as they are more or less of the same age group. Adoption experts say that exposure to different 'kinds' of people is important to give the adopted child an idea that she's part of a wider and more colourful spectrum. That way, even if there aren't any adopted kids in her immediate vicinity, she still knows that her school or playground isn't the beginning and end of the world—that there's a wider world out there and it is truly a rainbow of diversity.

Making Sense of Different Adoption Stories

Sunaina, Sudha and Purab's five-year-old adopted daughter, has grown up listening to the story of how her parents prayed to God so that He would send them a baby and that's how they came across the nuns at Missionaries of Charity who helped them find their daughter. Others, like single mum Ritu*, explained the concept of adoption to her daughter Megha* by telling her that she was 'chosen'. She told her that she had looked far and wide for the most beautiful daughter in the world and finally discovered her baby girl at the agency nursery. In our case, we have told Kiki that the good sisters at Missionaries helped Baba and Mamma find our little girl so we would have her to love and hold forever. We've not yet introduced the concept of babies from the heart because Kiki is still too young to understand.

Each set of adoptive parents has their own 'coming home' story with which they explain the adoption issue to their children. (See Chapter 4: Talking Adoption for a detailed treatment of the issue). It differs from parent to parent, and while networking with fellow adoptive parents I have found myself completely disagreeing with some of these stories. The question is if I allow my child to stay in touch socially with other adopted children, how do I explain different adoption stories that they may have grown up with? Particularly those that I can't relate to myself.

Adopted children who grow up with a particular homecoming story may find stories of other children confusing. When Jayanti introduced Kiki to Torsha and told her Kiki was also adopted like her, Torsha did not react too much. But her eyes lit up when her mother explained, 'She's another Palna baby.' Though Kiki is not from Palna, telling Torsha she was from another agency would have confused her even more. While discussing the homecoming stories of other adopted children, parents should keep this in mind. Rejigging another story to fit your own homecoming tale will make it both understandable and acceptable to the child.

The good thing is preschoolers or toddlers are too small to swap their homecoming stories. But by the time they can, they are also aware of the adoption issue or at least the word adoption and know that their parents were trying to explain it to them through the homecoming story.

8

The Legal Angle

TILL RECENTLY ADOPTION in India came under a maze of laws and hapless parents often had to fight both a sluggish system as well as a legal labyrinth. The legal hiccups could range from a lawyer who had absolutely no interest in spending time on what's essentially pro bono work, to knotty laws that disallow a couple from adopting a child of the same sex if they already have a biological child. In other words, if you have a daughter, you can't adopt a sister sibling for her. Before Kiki came home and for many months afterwards, we, like most adoptive parents, functioned in a kind of legal info vacuum. We blindly followed orders from the lawyer attached to our agency and luckily it all turned out fine for us. But not everyone is quite that lucky. So it makes eminent sense to get a hang of the laws that govern adoption in India.

Take Shonali and Arun who have recently become proud adoptive parents of a baby girl. Nearly a month after their baby came home, they became understandably worried that the legal procedure had not taken off. Their lawyer seemed indifferent at best and rude at worst. She behaved like she was doing them a favour and often would simply not even take their calls. 'Forget calls, she barely responded to our SMSs. It came to a point where we were getting her to work through our adoption officer who became our mediator,' says Shonali.

Shonali and Arun aren't the only ones to experience a faceoff with their lawyer. In Fabrise and Indira's* case, for example, the relationship with the lawyer became bitter enough for the latter to try and scupper their chances of getting their baby. 'He told us that we were not eligible because my husband is French and I am Indian,' remembers Indira. 'He even said if it was the other way round, it would have been okay.' The lawyer took a dislike to the couple in general and Indira's father in particular, and the relationship became 'unnecessarily fraught'. Fabrise and Indira tried everything to change the lawyer because the baby was still in the orphanage and Indira was still going across every day to see her. And then one fine morning she was simply told she couldn't see her baby. For the couple it was a bolt from the blue and they were understandably at the end of their tether. It took several rounds of fresh negotiations for the lawyer to finally back off and initiate the legal proceedings. As a result, the whole process got delayed by around four months.

Examples like these aren't uncommon. So what do you do if you come across a lawyer who is either dragging his feet or being stroppy about your case? Simple. You complain. Anu J. Singh, member secretary and chief executive officer of CARA, categorically says nothing much is done in terms of redressal because parents don't complain. 'CARA should get a complaint from the parents and then we can take it up either with the bar council or ask the agency to change the lawyer,' she says.

Similarly if any agency threatens prospective parents with blacklisting because of a breakdown in their relationship, the parents should immediately bring it to CARA's notice. 'There is no such thing as blacklisting,' says Singh. 'Most agencies do a great job and are invariably polite but if there are exceptions, parents should complain to CARA. No agency can blacklist a parent who is eligible.'

Adoption Laws

Currently there are three Acts which cover Indian adoptions. There is of course the Hindu Adoptions and Maintenance Act, 1956 (HAMA) under which Hindus,

Buddhists, Jains, and Sikhs can adopt. However, this Act does not cover Muslims, Christians, Parsis, and Jews. Nor does it cover any member of a Scheduled Tribe notified under the Constitution of India who is governed by their customary laws.

HAMA also dictates that only a Hindu, Buddhist, Sikh, or Jain 'husband' can adopt, with the consent of his wife. Single women can also adopt but a Hindu wife or legally separated woman cannot. HAMA also stipulates that the child being adopted should be a Hindu, either abandoned by his parents or whose parentage is unknown and who is less than fifteen years old. But most curiously it says that if the adoptive parent already has a biological daughter or granddaughter, he cannot adopt a girl. Similarly if he has a biological son or grandson, he can't adopt a boy. Besides, the age difference between parents and child must be at least twenty-one years. Senior advocate Geeta Luthra says HAMA is not the only option for Hindu adoptions. 'If a Hindu is adopting a relative, then it can be done through a datta honam (ceremony before the fire) and adoption deed,' she says. 'But if you are a Hindu and adopting from an orphanage, then it's mostly through HAMA.'

For non-Hindus, there are two options available for adoption. The first is the GAWA 1890. Under this Act, parents take over guardianship of the child as their ward. The guardian is responsible for the health, education, and support of the child as long as the child is a minor, says Dr Jagannath Pati, deputy director, CARA. Once the child attains eighteen years of age, the guardian and ward have no rights and responsibilities towards each other.

GAWA, says Luthra, is 'very unfair to the child'. Because HAMA is not a secular Act and adoptions by other communities like Christians and Muslims need to take their laws into account, many families have no option but to adopt under GAWA. Little Brigitte, Lancelot and Sheela Cutinha's youngest girl, for instance, was adopted under GAWA. The problem with GAWA is that the child does not get any inheritance rights and has no legal rights to child support from parents beyond eighteen years of age. Legally, the guardian's responsibility ends at that age. Parents will need to make special arrangements in the form of a will, for instance, if they want their child to inherit property or other valuables. GAWA is popular in overseas adoptions 'where children are taken with guardianship order by the foreign prospective adoptive parents and they are adopted as per their country laws', says Dr Pati.

The third Act governing adoptions is the Juvenile Justice (Care and Protection of Children) Act, 2000 as amended in 2006 (JJ Act). This is a secular Act and can cover both domestic as well as overseas adoptions by all communities. 'The JJ Act recognizes adoption and we are advising all agencies that parents should adopt under the JJ Act irrespective of religion because it is a secular Act,' says CARA CEO Anu J. Singh. In fact with the JJ Act becoming the umbrella Act for all adoptions, the confusion over multiple laws governing adoption by different types of parents from different communities has now been rectified. CARA's new adoption guidelines clearly say that all adoption of children 'in need of care and protection' shall proceed under the 'JJ Act which will ensure adequate safeguards for the adopted children', says Dr Pati. 'Already both in-country and inter-country adoption have started under the JJ Act.'

Advocate Geeta Luthra says the JJ Act covers two types of children—those who are in need of protection and those who have committed an infraction. 'Covering both under the same roof, as it were, is a problem area because one set has violated the law and the other needs protection from the law,' she says. Lawyers also say there could be a legal problem with the JJ Act superceding HAMA and GAWA which are both 'Acts of Parliament'. Luthra, though, says that should not be a legal problem as the JJ Act is also an Act of Parliament and 'its enactment is a centralized enactment'.

According to Dr Pati, in the case of adoption under the JJ Act the petitions can be filed under Section 41 of the Act. This section lays down the parameters for adoption and corrects many of the quirks in the HAMA Act. It says adoption will be resorted to for rehabilitation of children who are orphans, abandoned, or surrendered and that the court may allow a child to be given in adoption to a person regardless of marital status or to childless couples or allow parents to adopt a child of the same sex irrespective of the number of living biological sons or daughters. Indeed in a famous interpretation in 2009, the Bombay High Court clarified that where the child to be adopted falls within a description of an orphaned, abandoned, or surrendered child, the provisions of the JJ Act of 2000 must prevail. In such a case the embargo that is imposed on adopting a child of the same sex by a Hindu under HAMA, 1956 must give way to the salutary provisions made by the JJ Act. 'The apex court and different high courts have interpreted the JJ Act as an enabling/beneficial legislation,' says Dr Pati.

Rights of Birth Parents: Can these be Challenged?

Many of the parents I spoke to while researching for this book admitted that they spent some anxious moments wondering if their baby would be taken away from them while in foster care. Till they actually held the adoption deed in their hand, many like Jayanti would have recurrent nightmares of losing their baby to the birth parents. 'I would often wonder, what if her birth mother changed her mind? Will she be able to take my baby away from me?' remembers Jayanti. Adoptive parents also often wonder if the birth parents will have any legal rights on the child in the future.

Unlike the West, in India the birth parents have no right over the child once the adoption is complete. Under Section 41 of the JJ Act, the birth parents get up to two months to reconsider their decision in the case of surrendered children. That's why the youngest infants up for adoption in any agency are never less than two months old. Kiki, for instance, came home when she was two months and ten days old. Also, in case the child is old enough to understand and express his consent, no adoption can happen without his say-so.

This means that the birth parents cannot come back to claim the child legally surrendered beyond the two months' window available to them. Indeed in a ground-breaking case, *Laxmi Kant Pandey* v. *Union of India* (1985)—which has become the parameter for most overseas adoptions—Justice P.N. Bhagwati delivered a judgment where he clearly said:

> … notice of the application for guardianship of a child should in no case be published in the newspapers, because otherwise the biological parents would come to know who is the person taking the child in adoption and they might, with this knowledge, at any time be able to trace the whereabouts of the child and they may try to contact the child resulting in emotional and psychological disturbance for the child and the possibility cannot be ruled out that they may also attempt to extort money from the adoptive parents. No notice of the application should for the same reasons be issued to the biological parents and this is particularly important in case of an unwed mother who relinquished the child, for to disclose her name to the court or to give her notice would be highly embarrassing.

Two years later, the court expanded that judgment beyond foreign adoptive parents, saying the directive should also 'cover the cases where Hindu parents make an application under Section 9, sub-section (4) of the Hindu Adoptions and Maintenance Act, 1956. We would therefore clarify the direction given by us and direct that notice of an application under Section 9 sub-section (4) of the Hindu Adoptions and Maintenance Act, 1956 will also not be published in any newspaper...'

Adoption experts say it is imperative that parents go through a government-recognized agency to prevent blackmailing by the biological parents or the middleman who facilitated the adoption. Once the adoption is done as per law, it is irrevocable and a valid adoption cannot be either changed or cancelled. Advocate Geeta Luthra says she has handled cases where the validity of the adoption has been questioned but not the adoption itself. 'They can question if the adoption procedure was valid and legal or not. Some people have sought the declaration saying that there's some illegality in the adoption but the adoption itself cannot be cancelled,' she says.

Coming back to birth parents, once the period of reconsideration is over, they have no claims over the child even if the infant is then in foster care. Once the adoption deed is done, the child legally belongs to the adoptive parents and the birth parents are nowhere in the picture. Unless you have gone in for an illegal process of adoption, you have nothing to worry. Beware of going in for an illegal adoption in which you pay for your choice of baby. It is punishable by law. According to HAMA, any person giving or taking any payment or consideration shall be punishable with six months in jail or a fine or both.

Inheritance Issues

One of the biggest concerns of adoptive parents is whether the child will be able to inherit property and other valuables. Adoption lawyers say there is nothing to worry about on that score except when you have adopted under GAWA. Under HAMA, the adopted child has the right of collateral succession both on his adoptive mother as well as on his adoptive father's side.

Dr Pati says there are some parameters laid down under HAMA as well that clarify the question of inheritance. According to HAMA, no adoption, validly done, can be cancelled by the adoptive father or mother or any person. Similarly, the adopted child cannot renounce his status as the child of the adopted parents and return to the family of his birth. All ties of the child with the family of his birth shall be deemed to be severed from the date of adoption. HAMA also says the adoption will not affect the power of the adoptive father or mother to dispose of his or her property by transfer or by will as in the case of a biological child.

HAMA also lays down specific guidelines about children adopted within the family. For instance, there is a provision in HAMA which says the adopted child will continue to hold the property vested in her and also the obligation to maintain the relatives in the family of birth before her adoption. CARA officials clarify that this means that the birth parents in a within-the-family adoption have the right to will property to their child even after she has been adopted. The rights and obligations, in this clause, refer specifically to children adopted within the family like the younger brother adopting his older brother's biological child. Adoptions like these were very common earlier when there was some social resistance to adopting from an orphanage or home.

Under the JJ Act, on the other hand, inheritance is a given and it gives both the adopted and biological child equal rights over ancestral and other property, both movable and immovable. Under the JJ Act, the adoptive parents do not need to make any special provisions to ensure the inheritance of their adopted children. The adopted children automatically acquire equal rights along with their biological or adopted siblings.

For non-Hindu parents adopting under GAWA, however, special provisions have to be made to ensure the child gets her inheritance. Because GAWA only establishes guardianship and ward status, the child has no right of collateral succession from his adoptive parents. Indeed the rights and responsibilities on both sides end when the child turns eighteen! That's one of the reasons why CARA officials are now actively encouraging all adoptions to be legalized under the amended JJ Act. That way inheritance and other skews in GAWA can be avoided by adoptive parents.

Other Legal Issues

Advocate Geeta Luthra says that many of the adoption cases she has handled involved issues that have now been ironed out by the JJ Act. For instance, she handled a case involving six American adoptive parents, including a single parent and a little boy with special needs. The adoption was being handled by a Patna-based agency and the case dragged on for a couple of years. 'All the parents were adopting under GAWA and were going to legalize the process under American laws,' says Luthra. 'Those problems have now been taken care of by the JJ Act.' Indeed many overseas adoptions or adoptions involving at least one foreign parent residing in India are registered under the JJ Act.

Yet there are still areas which have not seen any change. For instance, CARA's guidelines clearly say same sex couples are not eligible for adoption. Of course if you are really desperate to have a baby, there's a way out. 'Same sex couples are not treated as couples by Indian law because India still has not legitimized gay or lesbian marriages,' says an adoption lawyer. 'But one of them can adopt as a single parent.' Though like all single parents, he will have to prove to the social worker during home study that there is a support structure that the parent can depend on.

As for discrimination against single parents, that's still work in progress for CARA. 'We have been talking to agencies about discrimination against single parents,' says Dr Pati. 'The law isn't old and mindsets need to change. But we don't impose on the agency. After all they are the best placed to take a call on what's best for the baby.'

9

Adopting an Older or Abused Child

ADOPTION OF OLDER children, kids with special needs, or abused children is not very common in India. The agencies I spoke to while researching for this book almost unanimously maintained that Indian adoptive parents, single or couple, do not show much interest especially in adopting kids who are looked upon as 'problem children'. In the West, though, it is a fairly common, and very laudable, trend, and the adoption of older children is widely prevalent there. It has been difficult to substantiate with Indian examples most of the learning gleaned on how to handle older or abused kids. However, as more and more urban parents look to adopt, the stigma attached to the abused child or the problem child will go away, and adopting older children or children with disabilities too will come to par in some time. Indeed during the course of my several visits to Missionaries of Charity, for example, I have come across slightly older children, often with medical problems, being adopted by non-resident Indian families. One particularly winsome boy, about five years old, had some congenital problems, the reason why he hadn't been adopted earlier. The agency took the responsibility of putting him through surgery and he recovered pretty quickly. Last I knew, he had flown off to Canada to join his new family of NRI parents. Such instances are slowly becoming commonplace but it is still rare for resident Indians to accept a child with serious disabilities.

An Older Child or as Young as Possible?

Do older children (toddlers, preschoolers, or school-going children), or even slightly older infants, take longer to get used to their new environment? Is it, therefore, a better idea to tell the agency that you would like an infant as young as possible? In our case, that's actually what we did. We were very clear that we wanted to experience the entire gamut of emotions as parents. We wanted to go through the ups and downs, the highs and lows of parenting, and short of labour pain, we didn't want to miss out on anything. So we requested the good sisters at Missionaries of Charity to please choose a baby as small as possible for us. When Kiki came home, she was just over two months old. We believe those early months of sleeplessness, anxiety, health scares, and the whole hog helped us bond with our baby. It was baptism by fire but by the time it was over and my baby entered toddlerhood, I never again doubted myself as a mother.

Our experience though is countered by several others who have opted for slightly older infants. In Sudha and Purab's case, for instance, they wanted and got a six-month-old girl child. The couple, who did not have any immediate family in Gurgaon and would therefore have to get by with domestic help, were chary of handling a very small infant. They felt, rightly, that babies adopted in their infancy may develop medical emergencies and felt a slightly older infant was a better bet. Their daughter, now five, is a fine little girl so I see nothing wrong with their decision.

The truth is that there are pros and cons to both options. And adoptive parents need to look at the complete picture vis-à-vis their own needs and preferences before taking a call. Of course some couples like Probir and Madhumita leave the entire decision to the agency. Unlike most parents, they did not specify even the age or sex of the baby—they left it all to the sisters at Missionaries of Charity. Madhumita's logic is that their child was 'fated' to be theirs so why specify. After all, when you conceive, you don't specify your preferences to the doctor, do you?

Some categories of parents, though, opt for an older child because it either helps get around a serpentine queue of waiting would-be parents or because their support structures mandate so. For instance, many single parents opt for an older child to get around the problem of a long wait or because their caregivers at home would prefer a toddler to an infant. That is particularly true of single fathers. Celebrity dancer Sandeep Soparkar made news when he became India's first single adoptive dad four years ago. His son Arjun, now nearly seven, was two and a half years old back then. In Mala and Anondo's case, following their separation Anondo visited several adoption agencies in Kolkata and even registered with one of them as a single parent. Though he is yet to get a baby, agencies have told him that he should opt for an older child. With an ailing mother at home, Anondo knows he will have to depend on domestic help to look after his child. He thinks an older infant or a toddler will be easier to handle for the entire family. A teacher himself, Anondo feels he is better equipped to handle a toddler, even one with behaviour problems. He understands that the older child will take longer to bond and 'fit in' but he feels, as a conscious parent, he will do a better job of parenting an older child than an infant.

The Abused Child/Problem Child

How can parents know their child has had an abusive past, and how do they handle such a child? According to Professor Dan Close, parents don't necessarily need to look too closely to know, instinctively, that their child may have suffered trauma or abuse. He says it's a good idea to check with the agency about the child's behaviour pattern. 'If he acted up in the institution, there's a good chance he'll act up at home,' he says. Agencies often underplay these behaviour patterns, thinking it may affect the child's chances of finding a good home. But parents, unprepared to handle such situations and wanting to do 'things right', may be overwhelmed by the task at hand.

Adoption experts say abused children often do not make eye contact. Many abused children also shun physical contact—they may even be threatened by it, if they suffered violence in the past. Children with behaviour problems will be manipulative and non-compliant, says Professor Close. Parents should realize that babies aren't born that way and if a child is showing these negative traits then he must have learnt them somehow.

Children who have been sexually abused may show an increased awareness about sexual acts inappropriate for their age. Abused girl children can also adopt seductive and overtly sexual behaviour in an attempt to control grown-ups and people in authority around her. Physically abused children will 'act out' till their parents react physically, with a slap for instance. It's their way of recreating a predictable pattern, no matter how harsh the pattern. Unpredictability and not knowing what to expect makes these kids even more insecure than they already are.

The biggest problem with adoptive parenting, not just in India but across the world, is that agencies typically spend more time making sure 'you're the right parent for the child' rather than preparing prospective parents for the job ahead. As a result parents are often baffled by the behaviour problems of an abused child; they simply don't know what to do. Allowing that child too much leniency in the name of love will not help—he will think he can get away with more and will likely test if he can. Worse, if there are other children in the household, they will get a similar message too.

So how do parents of abused children handle the situation? Professor Close suggests 'clear, flexible rules' that will ensure predictability and routine in the child's life. 'The parent cannot afford to be inconsistent. So don't be harsh but be firm and consistent. Set clear guidelines and cues and chalk out the consequences of breaking the rules. Parents *must* be kind but consistent.' (See sections below for more on handling behaviour issues of both older and abused children).

Easing the Adjustment of Older Kids

Is it really more difficult for an older child to fit into his adoptive household? Adoption experts say there are age 'bands' when children show heightened awareness of their environment. For instance, an infant in the one–four-week age band is not particularly aware of her surroundings. Babies in that age group are more concerned about their physical discomfort and needs like being hungry or wet and so on. In four–twelve weeks and six–twelve months, infants show greater awareness of sights and sounds around them. They notice changes, miss people, and therefore can quickly react when displaced.

When Kiki came home, the first two weeks were a particularly trying time for us. She cried all the time, felt obviously uncomfortable in my arms, and would only quieten down when I rocked her on my shoulders.

I didn't realize it then but obviously she was reacting to the new environment that she had suddenly been thrust into. She was being handled by strangers, in a surrounding she didn't recognize, and was cranky and anxious. Later things settled down and she soon got into a pattern of feed, sleep, and play that we could follow.

Like us, Pronnoy and Jayanti too wanted a child as small as possible. 'Actual bonding begins from four months—before that all that children understand is removal of discomfort,' says Jayanti. 'Identification begins at six months so we were happy our daughter came home at four months.' Like Kiki, their daughter Torsha too liked to be held up rather than cradled in Jayanti's arms. One possible explanation could be that the sound of their mum's heartbeat is a comforting rhythm for the child, enough to neutralize the transition anxiety.

A problem with slightly older infants is that it takes the parents a longer time to get over the under-nutrition or effects of institutional care in their earliest infancy. Madhumita and Probir's baby Preeti, for instance, was underweight when she came home at six months. It took concerted effort by her parents to get her weight up to the common median and though the girls are the same age, Preeti never became as chubby as Kiki was in her toddlerhood. Jayanti too faced a similar problem when the baby took months to show any discernible increase in weight. Later, her paediatrician said this was typical and that her daughter would 'catch up' eventually. 'He said to me, "You have to give her time to get over those four months she was away from you in the beginning,"' recollects Jayanti. Today an eight-year-old Torsha is plump enough to go off potato chips and other junk food on her own. A budding Odissi dancer, she knows she needs to be nimble to manage those intricate mudras on stage.

Though parents may not realize it, children—no matter what their age—show grief and anxiety over their displacement in various ways. Most parents, like us, tend to club everything under the tag 'baby is cranky', but there are several reasons why baby can become cranky. Very small infants, in the two–three month age bracket, can get cranky, lose sleep, lose appetite, and have colic pains, and other physical symptoms as a reaction to the change in their surroundings. Older infants and toddlers react by losing interest in food and play, excessive crying, falling ill, and often an emphatic refusal to smile. One way of getting around the shock of displacement and reducing the newness of the surrounding is to visit a child regularly at the agency before she actually comes home. Baby Lily's mother Pritha did just that—while the lawyer and the agency worked out the formalities, Pritha would visit her baby almost every day. That daily contact allowed mother and child to get used to each other—for the baby it was reassuring to have her mother's familiar face and smell around her when she finally moved home from the agency.

Adoption experts also say that initial cranky behaviour is the child's way of showing 'grief' and the older the child the more pronounced the feeling. Displacement is a huge loss for the child, particularly if she was close to whoever was taking care of her in the agency. Professor Dan Close says, 'It's massively difficult for older children to fit in and bond with their new families.' Even abused children or children used to very harsh circumstances in the orphanage search for a repetition of their earlier routine in their new lives. Professor Close has worked with adopted children and adoptive parents for more than three decades. The search for a familiar routine, he says, is the search for 'order and predictability'. It is important because it gives the displaced child a sense of security and control. Displacement and loss are critical issues that all adopted kids—but particularly older children—need to resolve in order to completely transition into their new lives. And telling them that they have been moved 'for their own good' may not help because it will trigger further feelings of insecurity, with the child wondering when he may be displaced again for his own good.

Adoption experts say parents need to allow older children to experience their grief or anger so that they can get it out of their systems and move on. Not externalizing that grief may lead to behaviour problems later on.

Older or Abused Children: Transition Tantrums

The sense of loss and dislocation suffered even by tiny infants has been discussed above. With slightly older infants and toddlers, the symptoms—crankiness, stomach upsets and fever, loss of appetite and so on—may be in addition to the occasional 'looking around' as the child searches for his birth parents or favourite caregiver at the agency, expecting them to come back. In preschoolers and schoolgoing children, the dislocation trauma may take the shape of angry outbursts, bouts of sullen silence, not wanting to be hugged by his new family members, refusing to stick to the dos and don'ts of the new household, screaming and talking back at parents, disruptive and occasionally even destructive or violent behaviour.

Adoption experts say older children may also, at some level, blame themselves for the dislocation. They may start believing that they 'lost' their birth parents or favourite caregivers because they were naughty or they did something wrong. They may also believe that they need to show their new parents just how naughty they can be so that if they have to be relocated again it should happen quickly. They may also hold back against expressing their feelings or developing attachments, thinking their new home and parents will be no more permanent than their birth parents or agency and caregivers.

Older adopted children often go through a period of perfect behaviour immediately after their relocation. The parents may think that the child has settled in quicker than anyone expected but this honeymoon may not last very long. Adoption experts say this is typically followed by a period of testing the limits. The child will test every instruction, rule, regulation, do and don't in his new household to see how far he can push the envelope. Often the testing period also coincides with the child's inability to accept his relocation. Having been moved once, he feels he can be moved again, back to where he came from. All he needs to do is try hard enough.

Apart from direct abuse in their pre-adoptive life, many adopted kids may also suffer from what Professor Close calls 'prenatal stress' or early trauma in the mother's womb and that too can cause tantrums and behaviour problems later on. Adoptive parents Sumit and Radhika Bawa agree that the reactions of children in various ages may differ but there could be some imprint of nature which adoptive parents simply cannot ignore. In their case, their now teenage daughter Trisha started her 'aggressive phase' in her very early teens. With hindsight, her parents now admit, 'You simply need to take the nature part of the story on board—there's no getting around that.' Trisha's unstable behaviour, which has now quietened down considerably as she moves out of her teens, was so disruptive that it made her parents agonize over whether they were handling things right.

Sometimes there might be some specific triggers for behavioural issues. Adoption experts say schoolgoing children may suffer anxiety over adapting to their new school environment apart from getting used to a new home environment. Many children from distressed backgrounds may have learning difficulties or attention deficiency problems and may find the rigours of school life daunting. Having to cope with change on multiple fronts can heighten the anxiety and insecurity of the child. And parents should be ready to handle 'acting out' behaviour as a result of that.

Handling a tantrum, no matter what the trigger, isn't easy. It can be exhausting as you try to calm down the child without losing your cool. But in my case I found it helped me handle the situation better if I could put a finger on the real reason behind the outburst—typically, Kiki would have one of her crying bouts if she was either sleepy or upset about something. For instance, recently she threw a tantrum when she returned from school expecting to see her father back home in Pondicherry from Delhi. His flight was delayed so he was running late but Kiki, who went to school that morning planning her day with Baba, couldn't understand the intricacies of flight timings. She calmed down when I held her close and told her that I knew she was upset about Baba not being home on time and that he would come but a little later.

Most adoption experts stress consistency as the most critical aspect of parenting a child with behavioural problems. Parents need to stick to their word, no matter how small the promise. So if Daddy and Mummy tell the child that they will be back home from work by 7 pm, they should make sure that they are. Children suffering from anxiety or trauma due to the relocation may start to question every single promise that they come across in their new life. To reassure them, parents need to show that they mean what they say, whether it is a question of returning home on time or never abandoning their newly adopted child.

Adoption specialist and author Lois Ruskai Melina suggests that one way of helping the child is to spend some designated time with him and get him to talk about his past trauma where he is allowed to express or sort out his feelings of anger, grief, or even denial. The child must know that it is okay to go through some of the negative emotions that he is feeling but he shouldn't let them take over his entire day and affect time with his family or friends in school. Parents can patiently explain that a 'solution hour' set aside every day will be the time for them to handle his emotional turmoil. He should also be reassured that his parents will hand-hold him all the way and that they love him and will be there for him always, no matter how impermanent his other relationships (with the birth parents or earlier caregivers) may have been. The parent should try to hold the child or have some physical contact with him as he talks about the past. The parents should simply hear the child out and not react with shock or disgust or embarrassment. That way the child gets a therapeutic session of unburdening himself and the parents get a better idea of just what kind of challenges they are dealing with.

Parents may also introduce 'cushions' to calm down a particularly anxious or troubled child. Surrounding him with soft, padded material and fabric that's smooth to the touch, introducing a security blanket, or figuring out some favourite toy or book that he's particularly attached to might help. Parents can have a detailed chat with the agency before the child comes home and even request them to allow the child to retain some of his possessions that he is close to. If that's not possible, then enquiring about his habits—many children need a favourite soft toy or security blanket when they go off to sleep, for instance—might also help. Parents can introduce an object like that if the original toy is not available.

Children, even those without a troubled past, can get extremely antsy while travelling. I still remember our first trip with Kiki when she was just a year old. We were going to Pondicherry for our annual holiday and she did not like the travelling very much. Worse, we forgot her favourite soft toy Woofus back home in Gurgaon. Kiki was uncontrollably cranky for one full day till I took her with me to a neighbourhood toy shop and she picked out another stuffed dog for herself. She hugged her new Woofus to sleep and felt so much better the next day that the rest of the holiday was an absolute dream.

Disruption in routine is not something most children take very well to. It's an adult thing to want to try out new things and check out new places. Children like doing the same things every day, watching a favourite film over and over again, and visiting a favourite park or restaurant again and again. For a child who has had a traumatic past, being dislocated is his worst nightmare come true. It makes him lose control over his surroundings and peaks his insecurity. Keeping that at the back of your mind will help you handle his tantrums better.

Discipline in the Household

Parents who adopt children who are older or have behaviour issues are often torn between doing the right thing and not being unnecessarily harsh to the child. A close friend of mine, who had to take in her sister's seven-year-old after his mum passed away, admitted that she found some of his habits plain shocking. Her sister was a single mum and she had been ailing for a while. So her son grew up without direct adult supervision for a couple of years. That has made him impervious to any domestic discipline and unwilling to listen to anyone. My friend was shocked to see that he would stay up till very late in the night watching television. He would watch all manner of programmes on the telly, not just cartoons. He refused to eat vegetables and would demand a burger as school tiffin every day. My friend knew that she needed to change some of the child's habits immediately because they were unhealthy and indisciplined. But she had no idea how to do it and not make the child feel unwanted and inferior.

Many older adopted kids or abused children have serious problems distinguishing right from wrong. If their orphanage was a particularly harsh place, they could have got punished for perfectly ordinary things like asking for more food or spending more time in the toilet. A child in such circumstances will not know what is acceptable and what is not in his new home. When he sees that his parents do not scold him for eating more or spending more time taking a bath, he may think he can do other stuff that fetched a punishment in the orphanage—like stealing money, swearing, or bullying other children.

Adoption experts say parents need to be firm about the rules in the household. The idea is to be kind to the child but firm—he should know that his parents love him enough not to make him do something that will be harmful in the long run. According to Professor Dan Close, unhealthy parenting is all about being harsh and inconsistent. A drug addict, for instance, may turn physically violent because of withdrawal symptoms. Or an alcoholic may turn abusive if there's no money to buy any more liquor. Abusive parents are known to offer liquor and even drugs to their children. Recently British papers reported a story about a three-year-old child who was treated for alcohol addiction, making him the youngest booze addict in that country. It seems he's been consuming alcohol in significant quantities for at least six months before the authorities had him hospitalized for withdrawal symptoms. Children exposed to such conditions are used to not only harsh but also unpredictable behaviour. They simply do not know what will trigger abuse from those in authority. The best way to put a routine in place is to emphasize the exact opposite of that abusive situation—through consistency and kindness.

Adoption experts say the consistency will be tested by the child who will want to see if he can get his way around by wearing out his parents. If the parents are consistent in their reaction, after a while the child will get the message about what is acceptable and what is not. Children typically, even abused ones, respect and prefer authority. It takes the variability out of their environment. Abused children like order, even if it is a harsh order. Which is why many kids adopted from orphanages in distressed surroundings tend to look for the order and iron-fisted routine of the orphanage even at home.

Unprepared for this behaviour, adoptive parents can (a) become inconsistent about the rules, relaxing them because the child is hungry, or unwell, or the parents simply feel terrible about what lay in his past or (b) choose their fights wrongly, putting greater emphasis on small issues and allowing bigger mistakes to go through. Professor Close says parents need to pick their fights carefully. Adoptive experts maintain choosing what to fight for is one of the most crucial elements of parenting a problem child. If, for instance, the parents are focused on making the child independent and responsible for his actions, they should allow him to go to school in dirty clothes or with untidy hair—and thus face the consequences—rather than butting heads with him while getting him ready for school on time. As long as the parents take responsibility for getting him ready, he will know that it's all up to them. But once it is his responsibility, then he faces the music if he's late for school or goes to school dirty and unkempt.

Handling a child with serious behaviour issues is an entirely different kettle of fish and parents will have ups and downs—more downs than ups initially—that are different from the usual parenting experience. The parent can't, for instance, expect any change in behaviour by simply saying, 'If you do that, Mummy or Daddy will be very upset with you' or 'That will make Mummy and Daddy very sad, please don't do it—it's wrong'. Mostly these tactics work well with preschoolers and toddlers but it won't work with a child who has suffered an abusive past. Reason: such a child will not form attachments easily and if he doesn't care about his parents, he won't care about how they feel if he does something wrong.

Adoption experts also say it may be helpful if, after every outburst, parents take time out to explain to the child that his behaviour is not right but do so in a way that does not make him feel unwanted. For instance, if he's used to spitting in public or at people, the parents can explain they understand no one had told him before that spitting in public or at people is not wrong but now that his parents are with him, they need to tell him that this is not correct behaviour. It may also help if parents can, through their communication, differentiate between the mistake and the child, explaining that they are angry or hurt or disappointed by the mistake he has made but will not stop loving the child as a result.

If the child is from a distressed background where education was not top priority, finds schoolwork a challenge, and refuses to attend classes as a result, parents will need to work on getting him to understand why going to school every day is important. This is more difficult in the case of older children. Typically, preschoolers or toddlers like playschool, for example, because it is a social environment for them. By the time they join junior school, going to school every day is already a part of their routine.

In a mixed household, parents need to make sure the rules are the same for everyone, including the newly adopted child. If there's any change in the rules for one, it will be tested out by the others as well. So if the rule is that the children will watch television for an hour before dinner, then everyone listens to it, no exceptions. However, the child with behaviour problems may need special help with schoolwork and extra hand-holding in getting used to his new surroundings and parents may need to explain to the other children in the household why they are spending more time and attention on their newly adopted sibling.

A 'solution hour' is something that parents of adopted teenagers also use to encourage an interface on troubling issues of identity and heritage. (See Chapter 5: Teen Tantrums). That way parents can separate the adoption question from all other issues and clearly point out to the child that she will not be allowed to manipulate a situation using the adoption angle. Raja and Sebanti, for instance, religiously followed the solution hour method while handling teenage tantrums from their adopted daughter Koel. In fact every time she'd say, 'You are only saying that because you are not really my parents,' her parents would reply, 'You want to discuss that, we will do so in the solution hour but right now this is about you not bunking classes and it has nothing to do with you being adopted or biological.'

Adoptive parents in general also have very high expectations of themselves. Since they necessarily place more emphasis on nurture over nature, they—and that includes me—believe that there's nothing a large dose of TLC will not take care of. But with an abused child or a child who has faced trauma early in life, sometimes just love is not enough. Parents need to know how to tailor their expectations of themselves and seek therapy and professional help when things get particularly difficult. Parents, for instance, may believe that doing things right and giving the child a lot of love will help him get over his learning difficulties or his separation grief. It may help make the child feel better but it won't solve the problem. By lowering expectations, both from themselves and the child, parents will be able to count their blessings, no matter how small. Instead of waiting for the newly adopted older child to get 90 per cent in his class test, the parents can congratulate themselves if he manages to settle down to his new routine enough to not want to walk out of class midway. Taking a reality check on his progress may help because the child may take a long time to both get over his feeling of loss and abandonment due to the relocation as well as gain enough confidence in his new surroundings to do better at school.

Bonding with the Child

For any adoptive parent, the bonding issue is a crucial one. Parents agonize over when the baby will start bonding with them and how quickly the sights and sounds and smells of her new home and parents will become the security blanket for the child. I must admit, I felt both good and bad when Kiki turned extra clingy when I went back to work after maternity leave. At six months she was old enough to recognize faces and she recognized mine and her father's better than anybody else's in the household. I had to slip away to work in the morning or she would cry and when I returned in the evening, she would often reward me with a smile. It made me feel good that my bonding with my baby was now strong enough for her to miss me as I missed her while at work. But I also worried about how quickly she would become independent and whether she'd turn out to be a clingy child for a much longer time.

Older children sometimes take a little longer to bond and the process is of course different for every child. There is not much difference between newborn and slightly older infants—both settle down fairly quickly and bond well even before the first year is over. But the issue gets trickier with older children, particularly preschoolers or even schoolgoing kids. The older adopted child will also need to be convinced that school is a fun place to be. Sharing notes, chatting about what happened during the day in school can also help parents and child bond.

In a mixed household, parents will need to be extra cautious in helping other siblings bond with the abused or older adopted child. Parents spending more time with the special child could make his siblings wonder if their position in the family and in their parents' affections is under threat. Siblings could feel insecure and parents will need to take that into account as well. Talking to them, roping them into the care and daily routine of the new child, getting their support from day one is crucial. This will help make the siblings aware of the challenges that could lie ahead and also ensure they don't grudge their new sibling the extra attention that he is attracting. And if the siblings join in at chat sessions about the new kid's day in school, it can be an effective and enjoyable 'family time' for everyone.

In the Bollywood movie *Mission Kashmir*, Sanjay Dutt's character, a police official, adopts a ten-year-old boy whose family was accidentally wiped out during an encounter in Kashmir. The boy is shown withdrawn and traumatized till his newly adopted father initiates a game of cricket—both father and son have a great time and that starts the beginning of their bonding. Bollywood is not known for its mature portrayal of issues like adoption but on this count the filmmaker may have had a point. Using a game of cricket or football to bond with the older adopted child is an age-old solution and it works. Both parents and child enjoy the game and both can later look back on the time spent together with pleasure—a memory that brings a smile is something to be cherished.

10

Single Parents

TALK TO SINGLE adoptive parents and they will tell you that the parenting process is actually easier for them. Reason: there's no conflict of opinion between the partners on parenting issues and single parents can't blame anyone else if things go wrong. Responsibility is focused on one parent, as is authority. And in a way it works. Of course nothing can compensate for a two-parent household because that's the societal norm and a child needs the love, affection, and support of both parents to really flower. Single adoptive parents say the biggest challenge they face is creating or building a support system that will kick in when they are unwell, overworked, absent, or anxious. Without that their effectiveness as a parent can come under serious threat.

How easy is it for singles to adopt in India? The law of the land makes it very clear that it does not discriminate between singles and couples when determining eligibility for adoption. Apart from the basic rule that single fathers do not get a baby girl and same sex couples are barred from adoption, there are no other special regulations regarding single adoptive parents. But the truth is that many agencies prefer couples to single parents.

According to CARA's newly released guidelines, a single parent has to be between 30 and 50 years old and if adopting a child in the 0–3 years age group, the single parent must not be older than 45. If the child is older than three years, the parent must not be more than 50 years old. Couples in live-in relationships are not eligible for adoption and a male single parent cannot adopt a baby girl. Also, in case the child is a special needs child, the case will be granted top priority under the new rules. That of course applies both for couples as well as single parents but is relevant for single parents in particular because many opt for older or special needs children in an attempt to jump the queue and improve their chances of becoming parents. However, CARA has now made it mandatory that the agency will have a detailed chat with the prospective parents explaining the needs of a special child so that the parents are prepared for the challenges that they may have to face.

Also, the prospective parent should furnish a divorce or legal separation decree, in case applicable, as part of the paperwork before taking the baby into foster care. Typically, home studies for single parents focus almost exclusively on the support structures that the parent boasts and a single parent is also required to submit a letter from a close relative stating that in case of any unforeseen circumstance the relative would look after the child, as part of the documentation. Single parents, particularly fathers, have a better chance of getting a baby if they opt for an older child or a special needs baby.

Handling Adoption

Is it more difficult for single parents to handle adoption? Single parents face a problem at the outset—dealing with the entire process and paperwork of adoption can be difficult to handle single-handedly. In the case of Rupali Mitra and her five-year-old daughter Ariana, the judge asked Rupali many pointed questions about both non-resident adoptive parents as well as single mums. What helped Rupali was that her work with NGOs in Bihar gave her enough field experience on the subject to make her really confident. In fact she chose her Pune-based agency because of its linkages with the organization she was working for. In hindsight it was a good decision because the legal system was more organized in Pune than it was in Delhi at that time and her work made her more aware of the complete legal process. Despite this, the entire process of moving from foster parent to legal parent status and getting the child's birth certificate from the municipal corporation took over a year and it was not till December 2007 that Ariana's papers were finally in order. For a single working parent, that running around can be a problem.

In my chats with several single adoptive parents, I came across a pattern—the home study makes sure you are very clear in your head about childcare and other support and the larger family buffer is always greeted as good news. Though most single parents in India say they are lucky to have the larger family support that makes life a lot easier, particularly in times of emergency, single parents also need to make extra provisions for childcare like opting for flexi timings or working from home and networking vigorously with other single adoptive parents who can act as a support group.

Take Ketaki* and her six-year-old adopted daughter Pipli*. Having her sister, brother-in-law, and their child almost next door has enabled this single working mother to make field trips outside the city which is imperative for her work. Though Ketaki has always had full-time help, Pipli doesn't feel lonely when her mum is travelling—she simply spends the night at what for her is a second home.

Like Ketaki, Rupali and her daughter Ariana depend a lot on their circle of friends for support. A career woman all her life, Rupali relocated from the US just before her daughter came home in August 2006. Since she was working with a multinational think tank at that time, she demanded and got maternity leave. But Rupali felt those three months weren't enough. Finally, she decided to work out of home for close to a year and financially was in a good enough place to be able to take that decision for the sake of her child. After a year of consultancy work, she joined her current job when the child was nearly two years old. Despite the amount of time and personal attention she was able to devote to parenting, Rupali still feels the pressure when she now has to travel for work. Her immediate family lives in Kolkata while she and her daughter are Gurgaon based. She's also lucky to have a close set of friends but then again everyone works so the buffer isn't as strong as she would like it to be. Rupali says these challenges are in fact generic to working parents. But the truth is it's even more critical for single ones.

Single parents are also typically extra focused on the financial aspect of the child's future, knowing that there's not much of a buffer for their baby. Mandira, for instance, is saving aggressively and has also signed up for a hefty life insurance policy that will pay her son enough to cover his education, should something happen to her. Indeed her biggest fear is that she will not be around to see her son graduate from shorts to business suits. All she wants is that she should be physically capable of looking after four-year-old Atri till he's old enough to do so himself. 'I know there's no one else looking out for him,' she says.

Explaining the One-parent Situation

Single adoptive parents have a double bill of explanations that they need to grapple with. Apart from talking about the biological versus adopted issue, they also need to explain the single-parent versus double-parent issue. And no matter how honest you are, you can be faced with a child's complete unwillingness to buy anything that's not de rigueur in his or her peer group.

Take the case of Mandira and her son Atri. Mandira separated from her husband a year after Atri came home, aged three months. The ensuing separation was a bitter one and Mandira's husband refused child support. A working mum, Mandira is still fighting for maintenance from her husband but the more difficult part is to explain to little Atri why his father no longer comes to see him or even calls. In a way, Atri blames both himself and his mother for what happened. Though he was very small when his father moved out, he still retains a vague memory and thinks he's responsible for making his father go away—that somehow he didn't measure up as a child. Now that he's going to kindergarten, Atri has taken to telling his classmates that his father works abroad and will come as soon as he can get leave. 'No matter how many times I explain to him that his father and I are no longer together and that I will now be both a mum and a dad to him, he still prefers this imaginary story,' says Mandira. Atri is still too small for Mandira to discuss the birth parent versus adoptive parent angle with him but she's understandably wary of how he will process that information.

Atri isn't a rarity. Rupali Mitra's daughter Ariana too has decided to invent a father she never had to begin with. Rupali initiated the story of adoption with Ariana extremely early on. She used a water filter ad on television to tell the story of how she and her daughter found each other. 'I always tell her that I never got married,' says Rupali. 'I had to because the concept of shaadi comes in early. So I told her exactly as it is.' Yet Ariana decided that it was better to tell her friends that her father had become a star in the sky rather than the truth. 'Ariana tells me, *"Maine to sub ko bol diya ki mera Papa star ban gaya...jaise filmon mein hota hai,"*' says Rupali. No matter how many times and in how many ways she explains the situation, Ariana still hasn't changed her story in school.

Rupali's solution is to seek out more single mums in Ariana's school or playgroup and socialize with them so her daughter will know that coming from a single-parent household is neither strange nor wrong. Though Ariana is still in denial mode and does not want to talk about the fact that she does not have a father, Rupali feels it will all get sorted out as she comes across more and more kids from diverse backgrounds in her social circle. Rupali's recipe for handling the single and adopted double bill is to be as reassuring about the whole topic as she possibly can. 'I don't get stressed about it and I am comfortable about being single, which I think is reassuring for her,' says Rupali.

Also, her very varied group of friends—couple parents, single parents, DINKs—she feels, should hopefully help her daughter deal with the questions that she'll face in school. Though most kids in school are from couple households and children desperately want to conform to what they view as normal, Rupali is convinced that exposing Ariana to a diverse universe will not only make her more confident but also enable a better explanation. The more examples she can cite, the better the chances that Ariana will accept the explanations. The good news for the duo is that Ariana's day care has a single mum and she is slowly, thanks to deliberate effort from her mother, building a community of friends who are from single-parent households.

Like Rupali, single mother Ritu also says the way to handle the 'whole situation' is to normalize it as far as possible. As sole decision-maker for her five-year-old daughter Megha, Ritu sometimes feels a bit overwhelmed. Ritu and her husband divorced two years after baby Megha came home. Unlike Atri, Megha's father has visiting rights and offers both child support and regular contact. But what hurts Megha is that he now has another family and a newborn child. 'She somehow feels he needed this new baby because he was not happy with her,' says Ritu.

Things get even more difficult when the adoptive single parent has to handle her child's grief in addition to her own feelings of anger and rejection. Ritu remembers battling enormous guilt in the initial days of the separation. She somehow felt she'd messed up as a parent, that she was diddling her child out of the kind of life she should have had, that losing a spouse was all her fault. In time, Ritu realized her own grief and anger were upsetting Megha all the more. 'I realized I needed time to get over it and she needed time to grieve and it was okay to do so,' remembers Ritu.

Today, like Rupali, Ritu depends on her wider circle of friends to make up a strong support system. For instance, Megha is the collective grandchild of the parents of her childless friends. That attention and affection has helped make up for the loss of a parent that, in Megha's case, happened after she came home.

Psychologists say adopted children can grieve for years for their birth parents when a disruption like death or divorce forces them to revisit the loss of a parent. Take the instance of a forty-year-old lady who called her agency in Delhi to enquire about her birth parents. She had recently lost her adopted parents and was suddenly feeling 'a void'. The agency did not have the relevant details like address or phone number. They did not even have a name. But the adoptee simply wanted the reassurance that somewhere she had one set of parents still looking out for her.

If they are old enough to understand their circumstances in case of divorce or separation, adopted children may create an imaginary world of their birth parents, thinking that they would not have been thus 'abandoned' had they been biological children.

Many single parents also say their adopted children try to block out any discussion of adoption even though the topic may not be new to them. In Ariana's case, she listens to her mother every time the adoption issue comes up but doesn't want to go down that road. She absorbs pretty much everything that is told to her but does not want to talk about it openly. In Atri's case, he simply thinks everyone in his class is adopted—he's too small to understand the difference between adopted and biological.

Adapting to a New Partner

Most single parents say their work and parenting take up so much time that there's simply no window left to invest in relationships. Rupali, for instance, says she's perfectly content with Ariana and has not really thought about what will happen if, down the road, she were to meet someone she wanted to share her life with. At any rate, she feels Ariana has a wide enough social circle and it's not a female only universe that she lives in. Though she doesn't rule it out, Rupali thinks it's entirely unlikely that their mum-and-daughter-unit-with-friends-around will change in the future.

As for Mandira, she is clear that any person who wishes to share her life will have to first become a part of her son's world. However, she also admits that being a single mum had turned her almost asocial immediately after her separation. For a while she wanted her friends to socialize with her son as well. 'We became a package deal, socially,' she jokes in hindsight. She thought of the two of them as a unit and friends happily obliged, making it impossible for her to carve out any me-time for herself. Now, three years on, she's less obsessive about spending every waking moment with her son. And with his social circle widening in school, Atri too is becoming independent. Mandira has changed enough to at least socialize sans her child and she's not averse to looking for a father for Atri. But there's no hurry. She says he can see how much she enjoys being a mum and an independent person. 'He knows I am cool,' she says. 'That helps.'

11

Biological and Adoptive Mixed Households

For years, my ex-colleague Namita*, mother of two lovely boys, had thought of adoption. Namita had always wanted a little girl and after two boys, separated by just a couple of years, she felt the family needed a girl child to make it complete. Part of her reasoning was also medical—Namita was already in her late thirties and wasn't sure she would be able to handle the strain of another pregnancy. She had talked about the possibility of adopting a sister with her sons and they were both completely on board with the idea. Still in junior school, they probably didn't understand the difference between a biological sibling and an adopted one. In the case of the Cutinhas, their two older biological daughters were so completely understanding that it helped their adopted sister Brigitte adapt to her new family almost instantly.

Yet with nine out of ten prospective adoptive parents I spoke to, the single most common reason behind the indecision about adoption is the chance that they may yet be able to have a biological child. Many agencies in fact ask the adoptive parents to provide a certificate of infertility though it is *not* mandated by law. Still others admit they prefer childless couples. Yet, increasingly, couples with biological children are also looking to adopt and many adoptive parents go on to have biological children as well. Brad and Angie's rainbow brood isn't just a Hollywood phenomenon.

Processes and Norms

Indian adoption laws clearly say that agencies should not discriminate between childless couples and couples with children, biological or adopted. The only criterion is that in the case of adopted children, all the legal paperwork and the adoption process must be complete before the couple register for another baby. Often, agencies that are happy with the way an adopted child shapes up in her new home suggest another baby to the parents. The sisters at the Missionaries of Charity, for instance, have asked me several times whether we are contemplating a sibling for Kiki. The sisters feel, rightly, that an only child—adopted or biological—can turn out lonely, particularly, as in Kiki's case, when she does not have cousins her age either. Also, knowing the credentials of a couple makes the agency confident that the parents will be able to look after a second child as well as the first. Many adoptive parents indeed go on to adopt more babies. Aside from the celebrity instance of Sushmita Sen, who has adopted two baby girls, and of course Hollywood star adoptives Angelina Jolie and Madonna, there are many more non-celeb parents who follow up an adoption with either a biological child or an adopted one. Baby Lily's parents, for instance, are already looking to adopt another baby.

CARA's guidelines say a couple looking to adopt a second time should furnish the adoption decree while registering for another baby. Also required is a written consent of the adopted or biological children if they are older than seven years. Foreign nationals too can adopt a second time from India, but only when the entire legal process for the first child is complete. The 'written consent' is an important item not merely because the introduction of another child will require the entire family to adapt to the newcomer but also because the newcomer will need to adapt to the new family.

Though the law does not discriminate between childless couples and couples with children, agencies do have their own shortlisting process and some of them prefer childless couples to those who already have children. The reason is that there's a huge mismatch between the number of children legally available for adoption and the queue of parents waiting to adopt and some agencies feel childless couples should have the first right to adopt followed by couples with children and single parents. It may be a good idea to check with the agency before you register whether they informally follow any such rule. One way of getting around that unwritten rule is to adopt twins. The law clearly says that the agency will not separate twins and agencies routinely ask couples, when they register, whether they are okay with the idea of raising twin babies. If you are up for it, adopting twins could be the best way to get around the lonely-only child syndrome. Of course if, like me, you're spooked by the physical and financial demands a set of twins will put on you, you may make your preference clear to the agency. After all, making sure the child grows up with enough economic security is a crucial part of parenting in the twenty-first century. And handling large families with multiple kids is never easy, adopted or otherwise.

Having Both Adopted and Biological Babies

Many adoptive parents I interviewed for this book wondered whether it was a good idea to have a biological baby as well. Or whether it would turn out to be too demanding emotionally. But couples who have gone through the experience of both adoptive and biological parenting say it's the best and healthiest combination possible.

Jayanti and Pronnoy had their biological son Raju* three years after their adopted daughter Torsha came home. Lancelot and Sheela Cutinha adopted Brigitte years after their two biological daughters were born—being late parents meant they were financially well off enough to have another child. In fact, before they got married Sheela had expressed her desire to adopt a child. But after having two biological daughters, almost back to back, the couple stopped talking about adoption as Lancelot's income from the Indian Air Force would not have supported a third child. Nine years later, an eye disability put paid to his career in the Air Force and he switched to a civilian career. As his disposable income started rising, it encouraged Sheela to broach the topic of adoption once again, during one of their visits to St Catherine's Home, an orphanage in Mumbai. 'The rest is history,' says Lancelot.

Mixed household parents say the adopted–biological combination works well both ways. While it offers the adopted child the emotional anchor of a sibling—crucial during teenage years or when troubling questions about identity pop up—it also makes the biological child in a way more responsible. Torsha's biological brother Raju is her knight in shining armour. Every time she faces any peer bias in school, he tells her he is there to 'bash up' anyone who makes his sister cry. Stick thin, Raju makes for an unlikely Galahad. But for his sister, he is the biggest support in an environment where the kids have to look after themselves—school. Raju's muscle flexing, laugh worthy to his parents, has actually helped. Torsha's peer group knows her brother will take up her cause if anybody says anything nasty to her.

Parents in mixed households say the children can have a positive influence on each other. In Varsha Bhatia's case, her adopted daughter is a go-getting extrovert while the older biological son is more relaxed and introverted. In their schoolgoing years, her daughter would routinely prod her brother to get out of the house on time so he wouldn't miss his school bus, for instance. 'They are totally different personality types,' says Bhatia. 'My son is so withdrawn that if the phone rings he would ask his sister to pick it up. Whereas my daughter is such an extrovert, she would forever tell her bhaiya to get out there and get things done.' In Torsha and Raju's case, Raju is the more aggressive of the two and Torsha has a calming influence on him. 'Our biological son is so much more difficult,' says Jayanti. 'He's more aggressive, has a bad temper, and I have had far more concerns about him than about her.' Typically, in any tense situation, whether involving her brother and parents or involving her parents, Torsha is invariably the stabilizing factor.

As for the emotional and physical demands of parenting, that's no different from any multiple child household. Jayanti, for instance, had a really bad pregnancy when she had Raju. Her daughter Torsha was a preschooler by then and the couple were anxious about how she would handle news of a baby brother. Pronnoy and she agonized over whether Torsha would feel in any way 'different' or 'discriminated against'. But when Raju was born, a tired, unwell, exhausted Jayanti realized she wasn't feeling particularly motherly towards her son. She began to bond with him much later—when he was big enough to be cuddled. With hindsight, she says her adoptive experience was much better than her biological one and she bonded faster with her daughter than with her son.

In fact Madhumita, who has an adopted daughter Preeti, says her mother had such a bad pregnancy with her and her sister, born within a year and a half of each other, that she fell seriously ill and couldn't breastfeed either of them. 'We were the last of five daughters and our mother's health did not permit her to be very physically involved during our infancy,' says Madhumita. Handling two children isn't any easier for biological parents than it is for adoptive ones. The emotional and physical strain of parenting is equal in both cases. So if you think you can handle more than one biological child, there's no reason why you can't handle a mixed household.

Indeed where adoptive parents can't—for medical, financial, or other reasons—adopt another child or have a biological sibling for their baby, they look to the immediate family to provide that buffer. In Preeti's case her adopted cousin Pompey and biological cousin Cookie* are her playmates and support system. Though Cookie doesn't live in the same city, she's very much the big sister. In fact her aunts were thrilled when she wrote an essay on family as part of her schoolwork where the opening line was about her two sisters Preeti and Pompey. Madhumita and her sisters feel this relationship will be the strongest one for all three girls. 'I think Pompey and Preeti will be the archetypal sisters—they will fight and make up and always stick with each other,' says Madhumita. 'We hope the three girls will continue to be friends and that Cookie will look after her kid sisters when they all grow up.'

Interracial adoptions work best when there are multiple children in the household, both adopted and biological. In Nancy Mulligan's family, for example, there are two adopted sisters and a biological brother. Nancy and her sister Fatima* were adopted from India and Sri Lanka respectively whereas their brother Ed* is biological. Nancy believes that while growing up, sharing her identity queries with a sister who was also going through the same emotions and identity crisis was particularly helpful. And having Ed around helped drive home the idea that families don't need to look the same to be able to bond and love.

Breaking the News

Discussing the advent of another child with the older biological or adopted children is important in mixed households. Siblings may justifiably feel 'neglected' as the attention shifts almost entirely to the new child, as they invariably do in any household, and get into a testing mode to see whether they still have their parents' attention (and affection). That situation isn't peculiar to mixed households—biological siblings often show the same kind of sibling jealousy. One four-year-old actually went around asking his mother's friends to please take his baby sister home with them. Another protested to his grandfather that he should not cuddle the newborn 'like everyone else'. 'At least Dadu should be only mine and not baby's,' was the logic of that five-year-old.

What can also trigger testing behaviour from children when a new baby is introduced is the increased focus on 'good behaviour' from parents. Grappling with a new baby and the demands of looking after an infant, parents will often expect the older child, adopted or biological, to be a paragon and to 'understand' that Daddy and Mummy are tired and busy with baby. That heightened expectation can also fuel rebellious behaviour which is as common among mixed households as it is among biological ones.

While child experts say some amount of jealousy is normal and shows the child is secure in his family surroundings to be able to express negative feelings, in mixed households it can give rise to questions of identity. Jayanti and Pronnoy's biggest worry when they were expecting their son Raju was how their adopted daughter Torsha would handle the situation. Jayanti expected questions on whether she too came from 'Mummy's tummy' and thought about how they would explain that their son 'came from my tummy and daughter came from my heart'.

One way of getting around that tension is to enlist the help and support of older siblings in 'looking after baby'.

Not only does it instil a sense of responsibility, it can also help the siblings bond. My mother, the eldest of five siblings, is closest to her youngest sister. Reason: the two are sixteen years apart and my mother practically brought her up. The bonds forged early can last a lifetime—something that children will grow up to cherish.

If the age difference between the siblings is more, the reaction to the new baby will also be different. When Lancelot and Sheela Cutinha decided to bring their adopted daughter Brigitte home, they had a long chat with their two biological daughters. 'The day I broached the topic of adopting a baby girl, my biological daughters were very excited and supportive,' recalls Lancelot. 'I can't remember any signs of resistance or jealousy and on the contrary, they have played the role of big sisters very well.'

For Varsha Bhatia, there was no other option but to explain the adopted–biological issue early on. Her biological son is older and as her daughter grew up 'she knew that there was a difference between how her brother came along and her', says Varsha. However, as parents the Bhatias waited till the questions came from their daughter before explaining things to her. 'She raised them when she felt the need and the questions came between three and half to seven years,' says

Varsha. 'When the questions came, we had to deal with them and explain things in terms that she would understand.' Later, as she grew up, she would raise the issue mostly to 'clarify and verify'.

The Bhatias used their larger friends' circle to drive home the point that you don't need to be related by blood in order to love someone. In India it is very common for children to adopt friends of their parents as uncles or aunts. The Bhatias used that reference to explain the biological–adopted issue to their daughter. 'We would often point out a favourite uncle or aunt among our circle of friends and tell her, "See, X is not a blood relative but you are so fond of him or her. What does that tell you?" Marriage too is not a blood bond, it is a vow. Adoption is like that—it is a vow to love and cherish the child forever,' says Varsha.

Adoption expert Vinita Bhargava says parents and children in mixed households will simply need to get their heads around the question, no matter how difficult it is. 'The words real and own will keep cropping up and it can be very hurtful,' she says. 'But one needs to deal with it and parents should allow the child to handle it and learn to deal with it in her own way.'

While many mixed households worry about how to explain that one of their children is adopted and the other isn't, the Cutinhas don't see it as a cause for concern. 'We had decided to tell her about her adoption right from the start, that is when she was old enough to understand,' says Lancelot. Though he has not thought of roping in the older kids to explain the issue to his adopted daughter Brigitte, he is not 'averse to partnering with my kids, if required, to resolve any dilemmas'. This is because, he says, they treat their kids like friends and repose a lot of trust in their judgement.

Avoiding Discrimination

Like any siblings, adopted and biological siblings also fight and adoption experts say parents should not be spooked by any manipulative words that the adopted or biological child may use to get their way around. I remember while growing up I would often use the 'you love Dada more because he's a boy' argument on my mother to push a point home or get my way. My brother did the same. He would in turn say, 'You love her more because she's smaller.' To her credit, my mother never paid any attention to either forms of coercion. It simply didn't work; but that didn't stop us from trying.

Adopted kids will also try the same tack. They will use the 'no one loves me because I am adopted' argument to get around parental rules. It's not unusual for the adopted child to turn around and tell her parents, 'You don't want to relax my curfew or let me go to that party or let me buy that dress because you don't love me as much as Bhaiya. After all he's your real son.' It can be tremendously hurtful and parents often give in, thinking that it will make the child understand that she's as precious as her biological sibling. But giving in to that kind of coercion is bad parenting. It disrupts the discipline in the house and can turn the authority hierarchy upside down. The biological child too may use the same argument, saying that his adopted sibling 'gets more attention'. All of this is just emotional blackmail and parents simply need to see it for what it is.

According to Vinita Bhargava, the best way to handle this kind of manipulative behaviour is to 'objectify the problem'. Parents have to firmly say that if you do something wrong, there will be consequences and those consequences are the same for you as well as for the biological sibling. In Varsha Bhatia's case, her self-willed adopted daughter broke more rules in her teenage years than the quieter biological son. So she would get more scoldings than her brother. 'We were fair in our heart to both our children but rules were rules and you needed to stick to them,' says Varsha. Vinita Bhargava says it's absolutely crucial that there's clarity about the rules in the house and the children should know that if you don't stick to them, you will be scolded; and the more you break the rules, the more the scolding and so on. Being adopted does not make you discipline-proof.

Western adoption experts say the best way to ensure discipline is to separate the issue of adoption from the trigger that causes the child to question her parents. For example, if your teenage daughter says you are not letting her go pubbing with her friends because she's not really your daughter and her birth mother would have understood her better, your response can be, 'If you want to talk about your birth mother and being adopted, we can do so but right now this is about whether you are allowed to go pubbing when underage, and you're not. The law doesn't allow it and we won't allow it, no matter what your friends and their parents may say.' Parents need to make it clear to the child that no matter how hurtful her comments, they simply cannot let her do something that is harmful. The idea, says Jayanti, is to explain to them that both kids, adopted and biological, have the same restrictions and will face the same disciplinary actions if they break the rules.

Sometimes what also helps is if the parents avoid over-parenting or conscious parenting. Take the Cutinhas, Lancelot and his wife Sheela. 'Unlike typical middle-class parents, who are constantly anxious about their kids' grades and progress in umpteen activities—swimming, dancing, Vedic math, and what have you—we are pretty cool,' says Lancelot. 'Maybe we are very lucky as Brigitte is not as demanding as other kids and she rarely throws tantrums. While we intend to give her the best opportunities we can afford, we are not overly anxious about not just Brigitte's progress but that of our other two biological kids as well.'

Not being conscious parents also takes the 'this is important' tag off the issue of adoption. Jayanti narrates with pride how one day she scolded her children for doing something extremely naughty. 'I was upset with both of them and shouted at them. I told them, "Why did I give birth to the two of you?"' Later, she realized that the scolding was an important lesson in more ways than one. It drove home the point that there was no positive discrimination in their household. And that the parents treat the two in exactly the same way—there's no difference.

Sibling Support

One of the biggest concerns of mixed households is whether the adopted and biological siblings will stand up for each other. And how to handle the situation if they don't. Typically, the mixed households I have interviewed for this book have shown that there's no difference between mixed and biological in how children react to their siblings. Yes, there will be a fair bit of jealousy, there will be manipulation, there will be rivalry, but there will also be support—public and private. Jayanti and Pronnoy recount with pride how their biological son Raju invariably stands up for his adopted big sister Torsha including taking on naysayers in school even though he's only a bottom-grader.

Indeed, mixed households actually often depend a lot on sibling support while planning a future for themselves. The Cutinhas, for example, believe that Brigitte's two biological sisters will always be there for her even when the parents are no longer around. Though Lancelot and Sheela are both quite fit and 'hope to be alive and economically productive till Brigitte at least finishes her studies', it gives them comfort that their 'older daughters have offered unconditional support to take over as parents in case of a contingency'.

Apart from support, siblings can also help make the adoption explanation less knotty. As has been mentioned earlier, Jayanti and Pronnoy, for instance, had for years celebrated two birthdays for Torsha—one with her friends at home and one with the kids at the adoption agency Palna. As she grew up and started to understand the adoption explanations, Torsha would often say she didn't like going to Palna any more. But her biological brother Raju's enthusiasm kept the tradition going. Raju openly says he's envious that his sister has two birthday parties instead of one. When Torsha said she didn't want to go for the Palna party, Raju simply said, 'No problem, I'll go.' That turned the Palna trip into a can't-miss event and helped Torsha change her mind.

Even after they grow up and have families of their own, mixed siblings can continue being an emotional support for each other. Take Nancy Mulligan. Part of a rainbow family, Nancy and her adopted sister Fatima are now married and divorced. Both have children. Their biological brother Ed is also married with a child. The three keep in touch with each other and the kids are good friends as cousins should be. Nancy and Fatima have often turned to big brother Ed for advice on financial and other matters. And while they have chosen Caucasian boyfriends and partners, their brother's wife is of Indian origin.

That buffer of a sibling can also help adjustment, particularly if you are adopting an older child. Adoption expert Lois Ruskai Melina says another child in the family can actually offer diversions in the form of play activities to an older adoptee and thus help 'make the transition easier'. Typically, she says, the resentment factor comes into play when the new child 'displaces' her sibling by being the youngest or the only girl or the only boy. In the case of the Cutinhas, for instance, the transition was so smooth because of the age difference between their two biological daughters and their adopted child. Since neither felt displaced, they were much more supportive of their new sibling.

Having a sibling in the family can be such a good buffer that parents often look for a favourite cousin to fill in the gap when they have an only child. And that's as true for adoptive as for biological parents. The parents of the trio of Preeti, Pompey, and Cookie—a mix of adopted and biological, cousins, best friends, and stand-in siblings—hope the relationship will endure when all three are grown up. That their bond will last a lifetime.

Appendix

Abbreviations

ACA	Adoption Coordinating Agency
AFAA	Authorised Foreign Adoption Agency
APNA	Alternative Parenting Network Association
BCG	Bacillus Calmette-Guérin
BERA	Brainstem Evoked Response Audiometry
CARA	Central Adoption Resource Authority
CMV	Cytomegalovirus
DINK	Dual Income, No Kids
FAE	Foetal Alcohol Effect
FAS	Foetal Alcohol Syndrome
GAWA	Guardians and Wards Act
HAMA	Hindu Adoptions and Maintenance Act
ICU	Intensive Care Unit
IFAFA	Indian Federation of Adoptive Families Associations
JJ Act	Juvenile Justice (Care and Protection of Children) Act

NOC	No Objection Certificate
SARA	State Adoption Resource Agency
SOFOSH	Society of Friends of Sassoon Hospital
TB	Tuberculosis
TLC	Tender Loving Care

A note on the author

Nandini Sengupta is an adoptive parent based in Pondicherry. She is a journalist by profession and has worked with *The Economic Times,* first in Kolkata and then in Delhi, for fifteen years. She is currently working with *The Times of India.* She and her husband adopted little Kiki in Delhi and moved to Pondicherry in 2010 in search of an alternative milieu for themselves and their child. *Babies from the Heart* is her first book.